What goes on tour, stays on tour, until now.

I0186367

Real Rugby Union Stories

By: Chris Miles

Disclaimer

Attention, dear reader! Before you embark on this wild journey through the scrums and tackles and pileups of rugby escapades, I caution you: you may need to fend off uncontrollable fits of laughter, the sudden urge to join a rugby team, and a newfound appreciation for the absurdity of life on and off the Rugby Union pitch. Remember, this book is based on lived adventures and the characters I introduce in the book are based on my real friends, but of course I have changed their names.

In the event you feel a sudden compulsion to step into the world of Rugby Union, please consult a rugby coach, a physiotherapist, or at least a sympathetic psychologist.

Now go ahead and dive into the chaos of our rugby adventures. May your sense of humour be as robust as a prop forward packing down in the scrum and your laughter as infectious as a well-executed dummy pass.

Crouch...touch...pause...engage.

Copyright

Copyright © 2024, David Christopher Miles All rights reserved.

All rights reserved. Apart from any permitted use under AUS copyright law, no part of this publication may be reproduced or transmitted in any form or by any means, electronic or mechanical, including photocopying, recording, or any information, storage, or retrieval system, without permission in writing from the publisher or under license from the Author.

Copyright Licensing Agency Limited. Printed in AUS for Develop A Player by Develop A Player.

ISBN-13: 978-0-6482745-6-8

Dedications

I dedicate this book to the fine gentlemen who have shared these adventures with me.

My children, who will learn a thing or two about their father once they have read these stories.

My actual brother, for being my great friend.

And to my incredible and understanding wife, whom I love and adore.

Adventures

Introduction

Step into the thrilling realm of Rugby Union, where mischief and mayhem unfold in a riotous symphony of shenanigans.

This book is based on real-life adventures throughout my Rugby career, filled with tales that will leave your concussed cerebrum wondering, "What the hell is going on in the insane world of rugby union"?

Strap on your athletic cup as we tunnel through the escapades and exploits that make rugby a hilarious and unforgettable experience for the daring souls who embark on them.

Welcome to my rugby stories that have stayed on tour, until now.

The reunion rugby match.

It had been over thirty years since we had last caught up and so with uncertainty that we would get the opportunity again, it was decided that we were going to have one last reunion rugby match on the Talybont Cardiff University pitches.

The e-mail exchanges had been frantic for months as the logistics of taking the field had not been straightforward.

With us all now in our fifties and not knowing if we still had the ability to run, yet alone possess the skills of our playing days, caution had been thrown to the wind, suitable medical insurance had been procured, and the match had been locked into the diary.

Scattered to all corners of the globe, the original Rugby team of nineteen ninety-two had risen to boardrooms and ministerial positions on three continents.

Esteemed gentlemen with degrees, awards of excellence and doctorates from leading universities, anyone not in the know might have mistaken us for shining examples of upstanding members of society.
Yet there was a past, that had remained silent.

We arrived in late spring. Some had flown in from overseas, some had come by train, and some had walked to the match as they still lived in the nation's capital.

As we met, there was the warm embrace of friends that had become as family, long lost mateship, and the re-kindling of brotherhood. It was like being in the all-encompassing embrace of a Welsh cuddle, commonly known as a cwtch.

We got changed into our rugby kit, pulling on our shorts and shirts that now barely covered our bellies which had grown considerably since entering middle age.

As we prepared to take the field, amongst the laughing and joking of camaraderie, a few bottles of spirits had been passed around with the invitation to have a 'few little drinks' for courage.

I held out a glass as Buster was pouring and he sent a generous measure of whisky my way that had the cup overflowing:

"Do you have a taller glass that I can put this in"?

He froze, a fear descended on his face, and he replied:

"Why do you want a tall glass"?

Story 1

The Tall Glass

Our saga unfolded in the rustic pubs of Cardiff City with enough Welsh ale to quench a dragon's fire.

It was time for the annual six nations rugby tournament, and filled with hope for the national side, we set out on our rugby pilgrimage through the streets of Cardiff towards the Principality stadium to take on the mighty Scottish.

In February's frosty embrace, twenty fearless men embarked on a quest to witness some good rugby, some good drinking, and some good mischief.

We decided to start at the top end of Queen Street and then work our way past the old castle and then down the famous Marry Street towards the stadium having a pint in each pub that was enroute.

For those familiar with Mary Street, attempting to drink a pint in each of the 50 pubs lining the legendary street is a feat as outrageous as trying to teach a whale to ride a bike.

Anyone brave enough to undertake this pub crawl would understand the sheer lunacy of the endeavor. But being the intrepid drinking companions we were, we figured it was better to try and fail gloriously than never to attempt the contest.

Now, why Cardiff decided to have so many pubs on the pilgrimage towards the rugby stadium is a mystery only their breweries can solve.

Our attempt at conquering this Welsh odyssey resulted in us staggering into the Brains brewery by early afternoon paralytically drunk and so the burden of blame for our lunacy should possibly be shared with the brewery cartel.

In every social rugby team, there is always one chap who is renowned for getting into trouble beyond his fair share in life.

In our team of rugby brothers, that man was Buster.

Standing at 6 foot 7 inches tall, and resembling a Wookiee, he had played a very high standard of rugby in the position of tight lock. Further, to being a man-mountain with excessive hair growth and pungent bodily odours, he also possessed the common sense of a dimwitted dodo.

Instead of holding back our alcoholism once we arrived at the brewery, we switched to drinking smaller, more lethal concoctions of top-shelf spirits, which was when things took a turn for the worse.

We worked our way through whiskies, gins, vodkas and even a Bacardi until we reached the Devil's own brew, known to mortals as sambuca.

Maybe it was by accident, or by diabolical design, but we worked out that you can set fire to sambuca before drinking it, and as it was such a cold day outside the pub, that seemed a sensible thing to do.

However, the escalation to attaching the flaming sambuca to my body was another of Buster's Darwinian ideas.

In response to Buster's insistency that I go first, I lit, and then attached the glass of flaming sambuca to my left nipple.

To be fair, the sobering effect of pain, and singed flesh, caught me somewhat off guard.

As the flaming drink latched onto my chest, a perfect vacuum formed around the rim of the glass, and my nipple was violently sucked inwards.

I was attached to the shot glass, an unpleasant sensation pulsating through my body: a violent mixture of pain, regret, and shame, but mostly pain.

As the burning sensation subsided, I was left with a dull ache as the blood from my chest was drawn into the glass lured in by the vacuum's charm. I glanced over at Buster, who was giggling like a mischievous scrumhalf and decided that revenge was now my only remaining course of action.

I yanked the glass free and with a hiss and a pop the vacuum broke and the smell of burned chest hair emanated into the air.

"Now drink it," came the instruction from Buster.

And with sweaty hands, I gulped down the glassful of hot, sticky liquid.

I was left with singed chest hair, and a permanent circular scar around my left nipple which remains to this day.

Faced with this humiliation, my thoughts turned to revenge.

"Right then," I said.

"It's your turn, you twat, but this time you have to attach the glass to your testicles!"

A hush fell over the brewery, and I could see real fear descend on his face.

Unbeknown to much of the crowd that had gathered in the pub to watch the stupidity was that Buster, in addition to being a six-foot-seven Bigfoot, was also gifted with huge man plumbs.

The crowd had swelled to sixty onlookers, and for those unaware of the serious safety risk, the majority of the pub's patrons saw this escalation challenge as a natural evolution of alcohol-fueled tomfoolery. To Buster, however, this development had struck a chord, for his bestial bollocks were now endangered.

Although a degenerate and lacking personal hygiene, Buster was no coward. After all, a bet is a bet.

As he dropped his trousers to reveal his man-plumbs, the sheer size of his nuts drew a gasp from the men and a swoon from the ladies. Cheers subsided as the realisation descended upon them that an infidel was about to willingly attach a fiery liquid to his manhood.

I returned from the bar with a tumblerful of six sambuca shots, and ready to play Russian roulette with his future ability to father children.

The look of fear in Buster's eyes was concerning. As with all practical jokes, there is a point that pushes the fun beyond hilarity to hospitalization and we had now reached those cross-roads.

The crowd held their breath.

As Buster lowered the glass between his testicles, his life flashed before his eyes, and he began to question the so-called friends that had brought him to this point in his life.

As the glass, now fully alight with the flaming sambuca, reached up and mischievously tormented his testicles, physics came out to play.

One of his huge testicles covered the entirety of the glass rim, forming a perfect vacuum and violently dragged both his testicles, and his dignity, to the bottom of the glass like a giant red octopus squeezing itself into a tiny dark cave, and there, the fiery sambuca held him in a vice-like grip.

Time slowed, and as the cheering from the onlooker subsided, I reminded Buster.

"You still have to drink the Sambuca, you idiot."

All eyes turned to Buster who stood motionless staring at the glass which was now holding his nuts hostage.

As Buster began to weigh up the predicament of how he was going to rescue his testicles from the bottom of the glass, the pain must have been excruciating.

He started to whimper.

To be fair, we were laughing too much to notice the blood had started to drain from his face and after five desperate minutes of him struggling with his scrotal incarceration, Buster passed out.

As his eyes rolled back, and still holding onto his genital jailer, the Wookiee toppled backwards through the crowd.

They parted like the red sea as he continued his journey towards the earth, much like the world tree of knowledge and wisdom being felled in a forest.

The laughter momentarily ceased as he lay on the cold stone floor, clutching the glass, lost in his own nightmare, before the uproarious laughter resumed.

Moments later, the poor fool came to his senses, and with tears rolling down his eyes, sweat on his brow, and a whimpering in his voice, he muttered:

"Mummy."

At this point, I understood that this practical joke may have gone a little too far and that Buster was mentally regressing, so I decided to step in to lend a hand.

I grasped the glass and started to pull, but my efforts only made the situation worse: with every tug of his nuts, he was drawn deeper inside.

"Please, get this off me," Buster was begging.

"Calm down you big baby, you only need one of your testicles, right?"

I tightened my grip once again, planting my left foot firmly against his chest. Just then, as if on cue, two police officers strolled into the pub, catching us in the midst of our impromptu embrace.

Even for the most seasoned of police officers, to witness a man with his manhood attached to a glass must have been a strange spectacle to see.

The pain and suffering in Buster's eyes were clear to the officers; however, the stupidity of the situation was perplexing, and they must have thought that it would require at least three detectives and potentially a coroner to decipher the motive.

You can only imagine what the police report would have said, which is why, after a moment to assess the situation, the enforcers of law and good judgement just shook their heads and walked back out of the pub, confused.

Attention turned back to Buster's suffering, and so with renewed gusto and vigor, I started to pull once more at his nut sack, intending on springing him from his predicament.

With a loud pop, his vivacious man-plumbs were released back into the wild to rapturous applause and cheering from the crowd, which drowned out his sobbing.

Unsurprisingly, the escalation of practical jokes that afternoon ended.

We contemplated the timely rescue of his testicles and also at the state of shock that had now descended over the poor man as he assessed the damage to his red and blistered man-plumbs.

In between his sobbing and tears he demanded retribution, but I reminded him that it was he who had started the game in the first place.

Furthermore, if he was stupid enough to set fire to alcohol while drunk and attach it to himself then no one could be blamed for the outcome, an undeniable logic that he reluctantly accepted.

Having not played a game of rugby for close to twenty years, it was evident that we had left our cardiovascular endurance unattended.

The ability to sprint the length of the field, score a try, and jog back were distant memories. The rough and tumble of contact could now not easily be brushed off and as such cramping and muscle spasms were popping up all over the team.

Our medical support was beckoned from the sidelines with an icy cold bucket of water and a bright yellow sponge and began administering the magical healing effects.

"Christ, that's cold," I exclaimed.

"Not as cold as that time you shut off our heating," he replied.

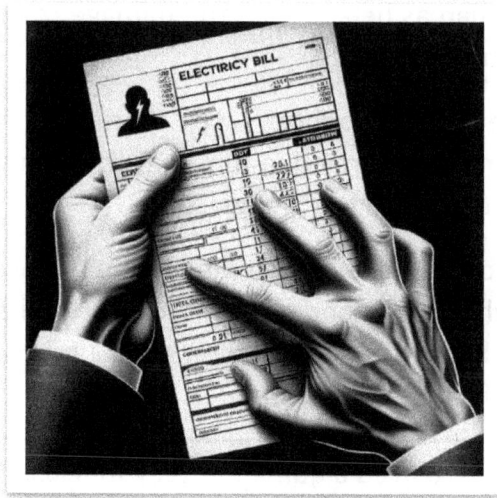

Story 2

Unpaid Bills

Back in the day, students who studied in the hallowed halls of the university moved away from their parents' homes instead of being cocooned in the warmth of their family embrace with the certainty of food and clean underpants.

So, when the official accommodation list was published, showcasing available houses that were practically indistinguishable from one another in their squalid state of disrepair, it was first come first served.

In comparison, if you were a landlord faced with a choice between five burly rugby players or four sweet young ladies to occupy your investment property, the decision was clear—unless, of course, you had a peculiar affinity for scrums in your living room.

So, when three mates and I secured one of the last remaining houses, 62 Colbourn Street—the last frontier on the university's accommodation list, we didn't quite know what to expect.

We had initially dreamt of epic house parties, filled with attractive models and a hangout for celebrities, but our hopes and dreams quickly disintegrated upon crossing the threshold of our new abode.

For the princely sum of one hundred and twenty pounds a month, we got what we paid for.

A bed, of some description, in each bedroom, a mangy couch in the living room, and a semi-functioning cooker and fridge in the kitchen. The shower spat out water of various temperatures, and the toilet just about flushed after jiggling the handle somewhat. But it was a palace of potential, a canvas upon which to paint our masterpiece of student living.

And just a street away at 58 Thesiger Street, a further bonus. My new friends Buster, Goldie, Jock, and Irish Timmy—comrades in the noble quest for academic excellence, or at least a memorable party.

As the academic year kicked off in September, so did the practical jokes between 62 Colborn and 58 Thesiger. Under the cloak of darkness, each household embarked on missions of hilarity, ringing doorbells at ungodly hours, stirring the entire house from its slumber.

As the weeks unfolded, our mischievous endeavours took on a life of their own. Goldie, in one stroke of genius, managed to copy my front door key and bestowed it upon a local tramp named Fred.

Fred, a man of delightful charm once you overlooked the scent of special VAT cider and cigarettes, would then turn up and let himself in, occasionally staying for the night on our couch.

But, for every action must be a reply, and so when I arrived home one evening to find my front door had been bricked up, 58 Thesiger Street must have known that the cold hand of revenge was coming.

Looking back on it, the jump in escalation from doorbells, tramps, and bricked-up doors to hypothermia is a leap but then again neither myself nor the lads at 58 Thesiger were prepared to de-escalate because we were having so much fun.

The calendar danced its merry way towards November, and as I arrived home, I was greeted by a figure that could only be described as Bigfoot's long-lost cousin whose DNA had been mingled with the Creature from the Black Lagoon.

A giant of a man with a wild beard and an overall unkempt appearance. My initial hypothesis leaned toward him being a mate of Fred, but I was wrong.

This behemoth was my landlord, and he had come for his biannual house inspection to see if the walls were still in place.

After some gruff instructions on the need for rat testing, my landlord, let's call him Billy the Beast, continued his inspection while I went to answer the knocking that was coming from the front door.

When I opened the door, another creature straight out of a fantasy novel stood before me, with one eye playing peek-a-boo amidst wild wisps of hair; I simply stood there not quite knowing what to say.

Even more of a mystery was that there were two young ladies, quite the contrast to our goblin-esque visitor standing by its side.

"Hello, can I help you"? I inquired politely,

 "Is my husband here"? the creature asked.

Assuming that some chap had done a runner and was currently being tracked down by the Goblin, I replied.

"No, sorry, no lost husband here."

A booming voice from the front room clarified the situation.

"It's okay, that's just my wife."

"Mary, take the kids home, I'll be there in 5 minutes. I'm just ensuring this house is OK before I check on the other one."

'Billy the Beast' came towards the front door, declaring all was in order with the house and asked if I could confirm in writing that he had completed his inspection and further provide written feedback that he was a 5-star landlord which he needed to maintain his coveted spot on the student accommodation list.

Still in contemplation over the genetic heritage of the afternoon's visitors, I said:

"Sure, no problem."

As he sauntered past me back onto the street, he paused for a moment.

"Oh, by the way, do you know the fellas at 58 Thesiger Street? I own that property as well and they're two months behind on rent."

"Nope, haven't a clue," I replied with feigned innocence.

"Ughh," he grunted and walked off.

And within the frosty recesses of my mind, a plan began to brew.

I sauntered over to Thesiger Street that evening to inform them of the afternoon's visitation by Billy, only to discover them huddled in the front room, lights dimmed, fixated on the TV. Their rent saga had woven its way into their lives since week one, forcing them into covert operations to avoid being seen using the front door. Instead, they opted for the ninja route—scaling the back wall and sneaking in under the cover of darkness.

As I laughed at their predicament, I decided to head back home where we at least had lights that could be turned on, but I was still thinking about what a good retaliatory joke could be to their latest prank.

Upon approaching their front door, I spotted their heating thermostat in the hallway. Slowly, with the precision of a mastermind, I unveiled the thermostat's inner workings. I twisted the dial down to an Arctic chill, then replaced the cover, slyly leaving the dial reading at a toasty maximum meaning that their central heating system would not be able to regulate the temperature within their household.

The result? A house perpetually freezing, with no heating in sight. Winter was coming, and my devious prank was in motion.

In the ensuing months, I became a regular visitor to the lads at 58 Thesiger. Clad in my thickest overcoat, I'd venture into their icy domain, only to find them huddled around the TV, clad in coats, hats, gloves, and scarves, trying valiantly to stave off the chill.

Their breath hung in the frigid air as they spoke, and, overcome with pity, I'd invite them over to my warm and cozy accommodation where I would offer them hot tea and biscuits.

"You're a lifesaver, mate," they'd declare. "Thank you for your kindness."

Despite a fleeting desire to confess my dastardly deed, during that particularly cold month of January, I kept the amusement going.

As the weather turned warmer by the month of March, I decided it was time to end the frozen saga. Five months without heating—a joke stretched just far enough to be funny but not too cruel, so I went to see them.

Once they had opened the door and let me in, I said:

"I've been pondering, chaps,"

"I'm studying electrical engineering, and in between the parties and the occasional lecture attendance, I happened upon one about control systems. It dawned on me—I might just have the fix for your heating system."

Hope danced in the eyes of Buster, Goldie, Jock, and Irish Timmy. A mate with a solution meant that the five months of near Arctic conditions and dodging the landlord's rent-hunting escapades could be coming to an end.

I walked over to the thermostatic controller and removed the cover. I slowly moved the dial from the revealed minimum setting to 'normal'. Behold! The boiler stirred to life, breathing warmth into the desolate property.

My dear friends looked on in stunned silence as confusion raced through their minds. On one hand there was sheer delight of having warmth return to their home but there was a nagging doubt that not all was being revealed.

I put the cover back on the thermostat and walked towards the door, leaving the lads grappling with the sudden shift in their frozen reality. As they stood there, still processing the miraculous resurrection of their heating, they began to connect the mental dots.

I had made a good twenty feet down the road, when the realization hit them like a ton of bricks, and pandemonium ensued.

"You bloody twat!" echoed the enraged cry from behind me.

"We could have frozen to death, you prick!"

Various other, less-than-polite expressions were hurled my way, but I was in full sprint mode, hindered only by tears of laughter and revenge dancing in the spring air.

> *As the game continued, so began the muscle cramps.*
>
> *A tube of 'deep heat' was beckoned from the sidelines by Scooter, a substance that is effective at warming up the skin, but less beneficial if you accidently get it in your eyes.*
>
> *As the liniment was smeared on his leg, he remarked:*
>
> *"Ooh, that's hot."*
>
> *"As hot as Fire Ox"? I inquired.*

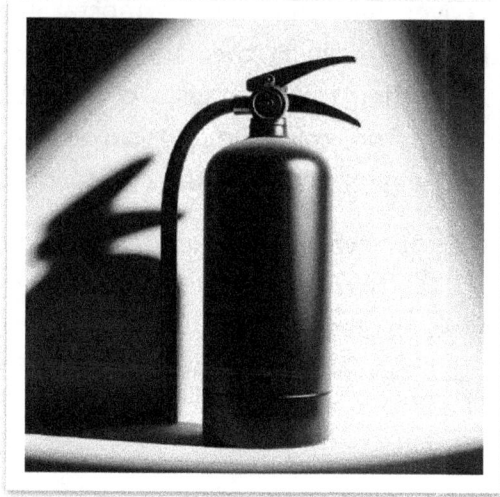

Chapter 3

Fire Ox

I have always had a passion in my heart and fire in my belly when it comes to rugby. Maybe it's because I am Welsh and having been born and bred in the county of Pembrokeshire, South Wales, it is in my blood.

Pembrokeshire is where the sun occasionally shines, but the sea is always blue. It has a stunning coastline, full of beauty and home to wildlife such as seals, dolphins, puffins, and Irishmen who just got lost on their way back home to Ireland.

But Pembrokeshire is so much more. It has a rich history of castles, cathedrals, druids and legends such as King Arthur and the Llangwm first fifteen rugby team. It's about singing, Welsh cakes, and hearty soup made with lamb and vegetables.

And if that's not enough to convince you of how wonderful Wales is, let me tell you about the women of Pembrokeshire. They are beautiful, smart, and fun-loving, and they adore rugby players.

Now, as well as being a budding rugby star, I also had a head for engineering. So, after leaving school at the age of sixteen and completing a four-year apprenticeship on the oil refineries, I made the choice to return to education and pursue a degree in electrical and electronic engineering.

I didn't want to stray too far from my beloved Pembrokeshire, and so when an opportunity presented itself to study at Cardiff University in the nineteen nineties, a mere hundred miles from home, I jumped at the chance.

Those were the days of crazy escapades; some of which you can read about in this book, but I also made a lifelong pal who I'll call 'Scooter' to protect his identity.

Scooter was a cheeky bloke from East London who had a knack for getting into trouble, but he was also a loyal and special mate who always had my back. We had some epic adventures together over the years and so when we got a chance to meet up again in Cardiff in 2007, we knew we were in for a blast.

After checking into a reasonably priced hotel in the centre of the city, we decided that we were going to start our reunion tour at the Tavern bar, which was in the Students Union. It also held so many memories of mischief from our time at university when we ruled the place through our legendary exploits, that it only made sense.

As we stood there at the bar, we recounted stories of drinking, ladies pursued, and mischief achieved. Trolling through the black book of memories with giggles and happiness, we also recalled one of our favorite drinking games which was called Tequila Stuntman.

Tequila Stuntman, for those unaware of its lethality, is the classic shot of tequila, salt and lemon but drunk in a special order to inflict maximum pain, blindness, and sensory deprivation.

Let me explain the process:

Firstly, you line up the salt and proceed to snort it up both your nostrils. Then, while the pain sends your olfactory canal into a flap, you quickly grab the shot of tequila and down it.

As you stand there in shock, with snot rolling down your face and the sensation of tequila burning its way towards your belly, you grab a slice of lemon and squeeze it in your eyes rendering yourself blind - just to prove to your mate that you can do stupid shit!

So, after several minutes of taking in the sights and sounds of our old university stomping ground, and reminiscing of good old days, we felt a need to relive our stupidity and once again consume a Tequila Stuntman, strapping ourselves in for a nonstop ride to oblivion.

As we stood there at the bar, waiting to be served our cocktail of doom, in barreled the current Cardiff University Rugby Team looking young and innocent and yet to sample the delights of Colliflower ears and split eyebrow from vigorous rucking.

A wry smile crept across Scooters face as one of the young men approached the bar and placed an order of drinks.

"15 tequilas, some salt and plenty of lemons, my good lady."

We watched in both disbelief and pride as each of these young chaps snorted their salt, downed the tequila, and then squeezed the lemon juice in their eyes without any prompting or explanation of the ritual.

I introduced myself to the only one of the players who was not currently coughing and crying like a baby, and I asked him where he learned to drink in such a magnificent way.

"You see," he started,

"it's a tradition of the Cardiff University Rugby team that this is the only way we drink tequila here."

"But who started this tradition"? I enquired

"Mate, a few years back, an absolute rugby legend named Milo, came through this fine university and taught us the way."

"Interesting," I replied and then turned to face Scooter who was gradually turning red in frustration.

"You absolute tosser!" Scooter blurted out.

"You know that both of us invented that game, I will be damned if you are going to get all the credit for that."

I reminded Scooter that I was always the brains of our duo, and he was just the token Englishman who had been included as part of an outreach program for the less fortunate.

We eventually left the Tavern safe in the knowledge that our drinking wisdom had been passed on to the next generation of undergraduate students, and made our way towards the lower end of the city.

As with all nights out in Cardiff everyone eventually ends up in Caroline Street, also known as chip alley, as it is renowned for the best Chicken Curry and Chips in the world. But before the inevitable munchies, I could sense that Scooter was still upset about the Tequila Stuntman legacy and so we stopped off in a swanky looking drinking emporium named 'Tiger-Tiger'.

Although 'Tiger-Tiger 'didn't have the rustic charms of many of the pubs in the center of Cardiff, it did however offer a wide selection of spirits in various strange looking bottle all on display behind a very plush and ultra trendy stainless-steel bar top.

As we took a seat, Scooter said:

"My good barman, we are here to invent a new drinking game and from the looks of your well-stocked bar, you are just the man who can help us in this mission."

The barman stood there not knowing what to do or say. Maybe because he was only a young chap and new to the job, or it was the glint of destiny Scooter had in his eyes, but he replied:

"OK, what would you like to start with?"

A malevolent grin spread across Scooters face as he began to instruct the poor naive barman on what needed to be poured into his cocktail shaker of delight.

For the next few hours, we sampled all manners of liqueurs and top-shelf spirits. There were bottles of green, bottles of blue, coconuts, avocados, Mara Chino cherries, and one or two fancy cocktail umbrellas.

As our cocktail experimentation continued, we arrived at our old friend Mr. Sambuca, and asked to barman to retrieve the tall bottle that was hiding at the back of the spirit's shelf.

"What's this?" the barman said.

"I've never seen that before."

Now those of you who are familiar with the lethality of Sambuca will know what a dangerous direction our journey took. For those unfamiliar with the Devil's juice, just like our poor barman, it is a clear liqueur with the added feature of being flammable.

"Two triple shots of that please."

At that stage of the evening, we were becoming slightly wobbly on our feet, and so when I stood up to drink my measure of Sambuca, I stumbled and accidentally spilled the drink all over the beautiful stainless-steel bar.

Disgusted with my heinous act of alcohol spillage, Scooter made a snap decision.

He picked up a match that was lying on the bar top and lit it. The barman starred at him in wonderment as Scooter casually threw it onto the liquid that was now spreading across the length of the bar.

As I regained focus from my stumble all I could now see were bright blue flames making their way towards me across the bar top.

Intent on making up for my indiscretion of alcohol spillage, I grasped one of the cocktail straws and started sucking up the sambuca that was not yet fully ablaze.

"Spoil sport!" came the cry from Scooter.

"You should have let that burn out.

"Well, you should not have set it on fire!"

"You stubborn ox."

The three of us stared at each other, contemplating the life-changing moment that we had just shared.

Scooter yelled out,

"Fire ox!"

We had found our new drink!

Inadvertently, we had discovered a new drinking game, full of theatrics, fire, and danger. The perfect game Scooter declared that we should introduce to the next generation of Cardiff University rugby players, and this time, it was he who would get the credit.

We decided to perfect the new game with a few more rounds, and even convinced the barman to join in the merriment, but when his manager came out to see what all the fuss was about and saw his employee setting fire to alcohol he had just poured on the new bar, we thought that it was time to leave.

As we left 'Tiger-Tiger' the night air hit us, and we started to feel decidedly drunk.

Chip alley was three or four streets away, and we both needed the bathroom to relieve ourselves from all the fiery liquid that was now in our blood stream.

We spotted the Rummer Tavern and decided that would be a good place to stop along our way.

The Rummer Tavern was a wonderfully quaint drinking establishment built in the 14th century, when merchants used to stop in for a lovely ale once they had unloaded their cargo onto the coal ships back in the day.

We stumbled into the rustic bar and used the bathroom before making our way up to the bar to have 'one for the road'.

It did not register at that point that instead of the modern décor as we had witnessed inside the 'tiger-tiger' bar, the Tavern by comparison, was more olde-worlde, and constructed from wooden beams steeped in centuries of alcohol and stories of adventure.

"And what would you gentlemen like to drink?" was the cheerful request from the lovely Welsh barmaid who had unfortunately chosen to work that evening.

"Two sambucas and a box of matches please," was the pleasantry offered by dear Scooter.

My eyes immediately locked onto his. Surely, he wasn't that stupid!

Once the drinks were poured, the barmaid wandered down to the other end of the bar, leaving us unsupervised.

Seizing on the opportunity to be irresponsible once more, Scooter poured his triple shot of sambuca onto the bar and handed me a straw before setting light to his end of the flammable liquid.

My reaction speed had slowed somewhat from earlier in the evening, and within mere seconds the flames from 'Fire-Ox' had made their way across the bar and started to climb the vertical beams towards the roof before I could start my straw-sucking.

I stared at Scooter, and calmly said:

"Well, I can't drink that now."

"Why not"? came his slurred questioning.

"Because it's too hot." I replied in a nonchalant manner.

A moment or two passed, as the two of us stared into the fire mesmerized as the cheeky flames began dancing their way up the wooden beams.

The bar lady looked over from the other end of the pub and screamed.

"Fire!"

Hearing these cries of distress, the burly bouncer, whom we had passed on the way into the establishment, sprang into life and started heading towards us with a fire extinguisher which he had ripped from the wall.

"Run! You bloody idiot!" Scooter shouted.

As we dashed towards the exit, we locked eyes with the bouncer as he ran towards the flames, it was clear that if his priority wasn't to extinguish the fire, we would have been in serious trouble.

We burst out of the door and headed off into the night leaving behind us yet another mess and carnage resulting from our drinking escapades.

As we stood there later that evening, having made our way to 'Chip Alley' and were tucking into the world's best chicken curry, chips, and gravy, we agreed on two very important facts.

Firstly, 'Fire-Ox' is an incredibly entertaining drinking game, which would be a great legacy to leave for generations of rugby teams to come.

Secondly, if you are going to play 'Fire-Ox' at a bar that is not fireproof, ensure the has access to a fire extinguisher.

With the game approaching half time and the lungs bursting from the lack of oxygen, player substitutions were occurring with increasing frequency.

Some were looking to stay on the field for as long as possible, and some were looking just experience the thrill of being on the field again with their mates.
A late arrival to the game though was Byson.

Cheers erupted has he took the field, not just because he was a man mountain of propping excellence, but because he had risen to legendary status back in the day, curtesy of an unlikely lady called 'Old Rosie'.

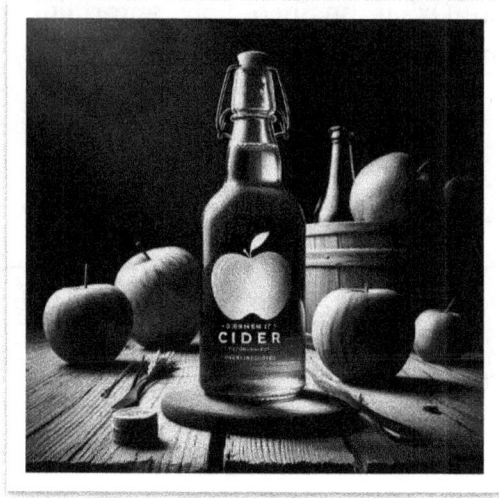

Story 4

Old Rosie

To imagine the Tavern bar, think about a 16th-century Gothic cathedral, populated by robbers and rogues: a quaint drinking hole filled with memorabilia of glorious adventures nailed to charred walls, its dark oak beams seeped in memories of misadventures above long drinking tables where mates would tell tall tales.

This small but satisfying drinking establishment became my second home throughout the 1990s, when I was not in my Engineering classes while studying at Cardiff University, and is a place that will forever remain a happy one in my heart.

During my rugby career, I drained many fine ales and had some fine evenings with finer friends.

And on strange evenings, when the moon was full and the inhibitions were low there was the occasional romantic embrace with dubious ladies from the town of Merthyr Tydfil, South Wales.

But by far the most extraordinary encounter came in the form of this story's protagonist, our guest from Somerset: the most unique and flavorsome 'Old Rosie Cider'.

The history of cider begins some 50 million years ago when it's believed the first apple trees began fruiting. Tragically, it would be a very long time before the first apple cider alcohol would be brewed.

It is recorded in the history books that cider was first discovered by Julius Caesar's troops in Britain in 55 BCE when they found the native Celts fermenting crab apples.

The Norman's contribution, however, was more profound; they cultivated a fondness for this ambrosia, adding depth and complexity to the beverage as well as giving the drink its name.

This alcoholic evolution to scrumpy came when unwanted apples were gathered off the ground and fermented recklessly, creating a more rough and potent concoction of murky mayhem.

Rosie Cider is a prime example of Herculean strength over flavour: at a whopping 8.4% ABV, it's no drink for the faint of heart. A cloudy mixture of desperation and wickedness, a cider that can dry out your mouth quicker than a tumble dryer set on high.

At first, it looks and tastes like lemon squash, so unsuspecting victims gulp at least half a pint before the unfortunate realisation that their legs have fallen asleep and their face has become numb.

Old Rosie first wrapped her arms around me when I finished a strenuous fitness training session the Friday before an important inter University Rugby match.

Having arrived at the Tavern sickeningly sober, I spotted the new addition to the regular lineup of guest ales and purchased a pint. The first gulp was refreshing, followed by a tart aftertaste, as pleasing as she was cheap.

As I stood at the bar, greeting fellow members of my rugby brothers, I began to feel a tingling in my lower limbs. Mistaking this sensation for the aftereffects of the fitness session, I brushed it off; but it soon became apparent that the loss of bodily coordination and morality was due to this newfound thirst quencher.

The next hour or so passed in a slight haze until I decided that I was rather hot and so unbuckled my trousers and stripped down to my underpants. On seeing the impromptu striptease, the part-time bouncers asked me to get dressed and head off home to sleep off the effects.

I had awoken some hours later, in the front living room of my student accommodation to find an eclectic mix of random objects: three half-eaten jumbo sausages on a plate, a bag of chips on top of the TV and two new traffic cones occupying the seats next to me.

As I sat there, trying to re-trace the journey in my head, I kept picturing images of apples in my mind, and so with a strong cup of coffee and a bite of one of the sausages, the Old Rosie image popped into my mind. And in that very moment, I hatched a mischievous challenge for our band of rugby brothers.

At the training session that next Monday night, I summoned the team and told them that we had a new adventure ahead. After the game on the coming Wednesday, we were going to assemble in the Tavern to have a competition and see if any member of the team could drink ten pints of Old Rosie.

"What's so special about that?" Henry, our Loose head Prop, boasted.

"I can drink that much in a couple of hours."

"Even Andy could manage six." Simon, our Flanker, added.

"Chalk me up for eight." Andy chimed in.

"Know your limits, you are just a Scrum Half, " came the reminder from Buster.

And the banter continued except for Byson, our neanderthal Tight head Prop, who just sat in the corner eating his post-match carbohydrate diet of six packets of chips and a whisky chaser. But there was an unusual grin on his face.

After some further debate, most of the lads thought that the idea had some merit, and so the challenge was on.

The upcoming game was a home fixture against Swansea University who were not a particularly strong rugby team, which meant that we were likely to return to the Tavern as winners, and as a result, be in good spirits for the drinking challenge.

And so, it was decided.

After the match we would all meet at the Tavern bar, each with ten pounds sterling in our pocket to purchase the liquid surprise, and on a mission to see if this drunken endeavor could be achieved.

As a precaution, we agreed that in addition to the funds to buy our own pints, all participants would wear custom dog tags. On one side were ten boxes to mark off each time a pint of Old Rosie was consumed, and on the other side was space to enter your name and place of residence so the ambulance knew where to drop you off after completing the challenge.

Doomsday had arrived, and we assembled at the University Rugby grounds for an early kick-off at 11 AM.

Swansea's Rugby team turned up in good numbers, with an expectation of an upset in the results. So, with copious strapping of ankles and liberal smearing of liniment on the legs, the match started on time.

It was a good first fifteen minutes with Swansea doing well to defend our back-line attack before we switched tactics and moved to a more dominant forward attack structure with strong runs off both scrum and lineout.

Predictably, we crossed the opposition's try line shortly afterwards from our well-practiced rolling maul, and ten minutes later, we were four scores up using the same tactic.

With the will of the opposition all but broken, our backline speedsters ran in some more tries from the wing.

In the changing rooms after the game, attention turned to our impending date with Old Rosie. An invitation was extended to the fine gentlemen of the opposition team, and although they were not pleased with their result on the playing field, they agreed to have a few after-match ales as is customary with the etiquette of the game.

News of the Old Rosie challenge had spread, and so when we arrived at the Tavern bar, there were already a dozen pints poured and waiting for us along with a small group of lady well-wishers from Merthyr Tydfil.

Even the Tavern's bouncers were intrigued to see if such a feat of drinking ten pints of scrumpy was even possible and so, purely out of curiosity, they informed us that they were there to support us in our mission of cider delight and not to prevent the merriment.

The challenge got underway with an almighty cheer and with one beer downed in record time, the atmosphere in the Tavern was electric.

Our rugby team had once again captured the minds of scientists who had come to hero-worship us, or at least study our intoxication experimentation.

To record the drunken progress, a tick was placed on the makeshift dog tags that hung around our necks, and more pints of Old Rosie were poured by the delightful barmaid who was now starting to look very desirable.

Old Rosie possesses an amazing ability: after the mischievous cider is consumed, it works its wicked way down the body, picking a fight with every organ, until arriving at the liver. Once at its intended destination, it proceeds to do all sorts of unmentionable carnage.

And while the body tries to choose if it should welcome this new visitor or deploy all its internal red blood cells to steel itself against the invading horrors, a second pint of cider flows down the oesophagus, which all but wins the battle for Old Rosie, and the body surrenders.

And as more of Old Rosie enters the bloodstream, the bodily functions yield, one by one. First to go is balance, followed by morals and good judgement, before the victim is left a jabbering, gibbering mess on the floor, clutching on to whatever strands of dignity are left.

Several pints into the challenge, I took a moment to look around the bar, and with blurry eyesight I saw, with both delight and horror, the carnage.

As far as the eye could see, there were rugby players in various stages of intoxication: some were fully dressed, some were partially dressed, and some were already in the fear of God.

Faced with my own impending doom, I pushed on hard. As the captain of the side, it was my duty to try and set an example of drinking prowess.

However, with six pints down, and only partial vision left in my left eye, I realised that making it to the full ten pints of Old Rosie was now beyond my mortal capabilities.

I held strong through to the bottom of my 7th pint before slumping to the ground, half-crying and half-laughing.

And as I lay there, drifting off into oblivion, I witnessed a miracle.

Our Tight head Prop, Mr. Byson, had risen from the ranks of the new man at the University to a demigod.

As he held up his 10th and final pint of Old Rosie and downed the entire beverage in one almighty gulp, cheers rang out. Whoops and whistles echoed throughout the pub.

Not only had Byson managed to finish the drinking challenge, but he had now found himself to be the object of desire from the barmaid, who was, by strange coincidence, from Merthyr Tydfil, and she was ready to claim her prized man.

As Miss Merthyr Tydfil grabbed hold of Byson, sparks of romance filled the air.

The two lovers left the Tavern in a whirlwind of snogging, intending no doubt on procreation, the like of which even renowned zoologist Sir David Attenborough would have been intrigued to witness.

Of all the fine men who had attempted the challenge that night, only one had succeeded.

As I awoke that following morning with a splitting headache, I was confused but strangely calmed by the fact that two more traffic cones had subsequently appeared at some point during the evening escapades and there was another bag of chips waiting for me on top of the TV.

After some self-reflection, pity, and fear that my liver had been pushed past the point of no repair, the events of the evening started to return to me and the achievements of Byson.

Now, as Byson only lived three doors down from me on the same street, I thought I would crawl over there and find out what happened after he had taken home the most beautiful Miss Murther Tydfil.

I knocked on the door and it was eventually opened by Byson's housemate; he informed me that he had not seen him since he had left that previous evening. It occurred to me that he might still be in the clutches of his newfound love, and so I started to walk back to my waiting sausages via the corner shop to pick up some tomato ketchup for the chips that were also waiting for me.

As I headed towards the shop, blurry and dehydrated, I saw Byson. Some 20 meters away, wandering in the middle of the road.

He had his trousers in one hand and in the other he held his stained T-shirt.

"Good God, man," I declared.

"What the hell has happened to you?"

Byson looked at me and shook his head before beginning to whimper. I put an arm around him and steered him towards the nearby café.

I took off my jumper and lent it to him.

"What's wrong with him?" asked the waitress.

"Not sure yet I think he's Murther Tydfil'd."

"Yeh, you could be right, he looks proper messed up."

"Cup of tea?"

"Yes please, and two bacon sandwiches."

"Tidy, coming right up."

I let him contemplate his life's decisions for a good five minutes before I asked him if he needed an ambulance, an undertaker, or a priest.

"All three," he replied.

"Tell me everything, it can't be that bad, can it?"

"Well, after I left the Tavern, I was feeling great."

"Yeh, I know, you were the only one to complete the 10-pint challenge."

"10 pints of what?"

"Old Rosie cider. Do you remember?"

"I can remember taking home this beautiful lady who was impressed with my good looks and charm."

The poor man obviously was very confused, as although he was a great prop, he was no Brad Pitt.

"She saw my inner beauty."

"Really?"

"But something happened, and I don't think she wants to see me again."

"Hell. What did you do?"

The story that Byson shared with me that fateful Thursday morning over a cup of tea was of such magnitude that I had to share it.

On arriving at Miss Murther Tydfil's residence, she had declared that she was going to do such naughty things to him, that it had gotten him sexually aroused.

But, as he started to get an erection, the blood that had been protecting his vital organs from the wickedness of Old Rosie started flowing towards his cock in readiness for the upcoming battle against erectile dysfunction.

And in that moment, all his other organs had shut down.

As Miss Murther Tydfil opened the door to her cave of carnal delights, dear Byson simultaneously vomited, peed, and shit himself in the same moment, leaving him frozen and unable to think.

And as he had stood there, trying to work out what the hell had just happened, Miss Merthyr Tydfil had concluded that he was not in fact her Prince Charming and duly pushed him out of the door where he had then collapsed.

And there he had stayed all night, asleep on the front lawn, before being awoken by a passing police officer and questioned for vagrancy.

As we sat in silence, me slightly giggling to myself, we started to reflect on the evening's adventure.

We stayed in the café for another twenty minutes contemplating life before the other patrons started to complain about the smell now coming from Byson. We stood up from our seats and slowly made our way back home with Byson letting out a small whimper every few minutes.

A broken man, a soiled pair of trousers and an encounter the queen of ciders. This was and epic tale that needed to be remembered.

With half time over, and the effects of another strong whisky in the blood stream kicking in, we ran back onto the field with a renewed determination to make it through the second half.

The stupidity of event was now evident with most players under running repairs.

There were men with bandages wrapped around heads, ice packs on knees and bodies strapped to stretchers as they were carried from the battlefield. Goldie, to inspire a defensive line yelled out:

"Come on lads, stick together."

He looked over at me and we both started to giggle.

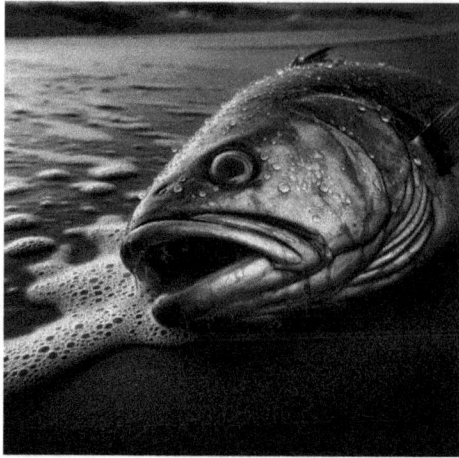

Story 5

I Would Not Recommend the Fish

In the early 2000s, my two very good friends and I, whom we will call Micky and Timmy to protect their innocence, headed to Thailand following the completion of our university degrees.

We had all secured Australian rugby contracts and were thoroughly excited about furthering our rugby skills on the other side of the world. However, after three years of university study, we felt that first we needed to blow off some steam and therefore decided to stop off in the Far East on our way south to taste the exotic and indulgent fruits of foreign lands.

We had briefly researched the various airlines and routes that were available to transport us on our merry journey but had decided in the end to fly with Finnair, primarily because we were expecting the flight to be crewed by beautiful young blonde-haired models who would be amenable to our Welsh charm and handsome good looks.

Whereas the flight was indeed crewed by blonde airhostesses, they seemed impervious to our best pickup lines and offers of romantic embraces at 40,000 feet, and so we settled into the flight intend on trying to consume as much free vodka as we could.

Blurry eyed and with thumping headache we awoke just in time to see the lights of Bangkok as we descended into the city of sin in the early hours of that Saturday morning and prepared ourselves for the mischief ahead.

Micky, Timmy, and I dropped our bags off at our pre-booked two-star accommodation in the district of Patpong, and we headed straight into the nearest gentlemen's club which was filled with all manners of temptation, mischief, and table tennis.

We were most fortunate that evening to have found our way into the Bada Bing Gogo Bar, which was visible by the twenty or so neon signs informing us that we were in the right place for fun but most assuredly free from venereal diseases.

And so, we entered the lair.

The inside of the bar was most curious, with scantily clad ladies prancing up and down a long stage running down the centre of the room.

Having just completed the fifteen-hour Finnair flight, and not yet had the opportunity to relieve my bladder of all the vodka I had to growing need to tinkle, so I excused myself from the impending catastrophe of carnal lust and wandered to the back of the club for my first encounter with an Asian toilet.

It was not the most pleasant of restrooms, and those of you who have visited the Bada Bing Gogo Bar can understand that the odor, like herpes, stays with you forever.

Nevertheless, holding back the desire to retch, I decided to remove both my shorts and my underpants to avoid any potential mishap or incorrect use. I bent down, stared into the abyss, and surrendered to nature.

However awful this particular Asian squat toilet seemed at the time; it was luxurious compared to the throne at the heart of this story. But before we get to that, there was more adventuring to be done in Bada Bing.

After what seemed like an eternity perched over the pit of darkness, pondering what lay beneath my naked ass, I eventually gave in to nature and relieved myself. Squaring away my undercarriage, and putting back on my lucky Welsh dragon underpants, I headed back into the main part of the lively room only to find Micky and Timmy sitting at a round island bar with odd-looking smiles on their faces.

As I took a seat next to my partners in crime, I sensed something was wrong due to the strange and strained expressions that the lads had on their faces. I turned to Timmy and asked him why he was wearing such a peculiar expression.

He slowly turned his head to me, and with a bright glowing face, and excitement in his voice, he said.

"I love Bangkok."

Unbeknown to me, both he and Micky were receiving blow jobs from beneath the bar where a glory hole had been strategically positioned. And while I was in the bathroom struggling with my underpants, my travelling companions had wasted no time in embracing the carnal pleasures of the Bada Bing Gogo Bar.

Following sixty seconds of contemplation, and driven by the fear of missing out, I decided that when in Thailand, you should do like the Thai do, and so my penis and I decided to join in on the adventure.

As I sat there, awaiting my Asian pleasure, it became apparent that this house of illicit delights had only two attendees: meaning that I had a hole, but not much glory.

I was quite disappointed, to say the least, which my travelling companions found hilarious, as they pointed out my inability to attract the ladies even in an establishment of this nature which made me feel flaccid, in more ways than one.

Jealousy is a powerful ally when considering opportunistic revenge. While my comrades sat there at the bar, sipping on their tiger beer, and enjoying the delights of the Far East, I decided to mount full-on psychological warfare.

"How do you know it's a woman?" I asked.

"How do you know it's a woman," he scoffed. "By her teats!"

"No, I mean... On your balls."

"My balls? What's on my balls"?

"Me!" a fabulous androgenic voice piped up from beneath the table.

Their smiles and jeering at my misfortune came to a sudden halt, as the realisation set upon them that they had not seen who or what was pleasuring them in such XY-chromosomal ways.

"The Bada Bing Gogo Bar is an equal opportunity employer, and ladyboys have the same working rights as breasted people."

"Isn't that right, Elton?" I called out as I gently knocked on the table.

"You tell him, sister!" the reply came from the burly sex worker.

Time froze, and as a smile spread across my face, the realization dawned on my comrades.

Timmy drew back his appendage from the inglorious hole and scrambled to pull his trousers up from around his ankles.

I looked over at Micky.

"What"? he asked.

"You deadbeat." I barked.

"What goes on tour, stays on tour." He replied and then continued to sip his beer.

After several days in the city of Bangkok, we decided that it was time to continue our journey south in search of other adventures.

We travelled third class on the Thai train network in the hope of embracing far eastern culture, which we immediately regretted after several hours travelling with live poultry.

We eventually arrived at the small port of Ban Na Bo where we had planned to take a small boat over to the Island of Koh Samui Island and there we had planned to learn how to scuba-dive and maybe take in an authentic Tai boxing tournament.

On the boat over to Koh Samui, we had some steamed rice and vegetables, accompanied by an exotic technicolored fish of unknown origins, and although the fish looked delightful on the outside, it contained horrors within.

After several tiger beers to wash down the meal, we arrived on the island in good cheer and dropped off our bags at the three-star backpacker's accommodation, which had been recommended to us by our boat captain.

To be fair, the accommodation was quite good, and a very comfortable three-bed apartment had been made available for us.

Spirits were high, and we were excited to see our first Muay Thai boxing match which was scheduled for that evening down at the other end of the island. I showered and changed, putting on my lucky underpants and a new T-shirt before heading out of the hostel with Micky and Timmy towards the boxing ring, a journey I would never complete.

Between where we were staying at the hostel and the boxing ring, there were some 'very posh' restaurants that had hundreds of revelers and diners enjoying all the Far East's flavors. Joyful music filled the air and there was a buzz of excitement for the evening ahead.

The moment I stepped onto the road and headed off towards the boxing ring, my stomach growled like a hellhound.

Something was wrong with my lower intestine, and I would need the assistance of a bathroom in the very, very near future.

Even though the hostel was no more than a hundred metres away, my need for a toilet was more immediate than the time it would have taken me to sprint back there, so I waddled up to the nearest restaurant and looked for the loo.

I made a beeline for the toilet, which was located at the back of the establishment, and made my way through the packed restaurant bumping into chairs and staff as the doomsday clock ticked increasingly faster.

When I opened the door, before me was a squat toilet much more rustic than the one I had experienced in the Bada Bing Gogo Bar in the aptly named city of Bangkok.

As my stomach growled again and the sweat started pouring off my brow, my anus clenched, restraining the torrents of evil that were ready to explode like Pandora's Box.

Taking my life in my hand, I bent down and whipped off my shorts as my stomach began to fizz. I was now dripping in perspiration, and the mounting pain in my stomach was reaching a climax, like Timmy almost did at the glory hole.

My relief was now in sight: all I had to do was remove my lucky underpants before achieving gastric salvation.

But the evils within the technicolor fish of unknown origins was not to be denied its victim, and so as I prepared for the final move of turning and squatting over the toilet, my sphincter surrendered.

As I pivoted over the squat bog, my bottom burst, and I began to spray my deadly liquid with such force it knocked over the decorative plants which had been lovingly placed on the wall of the bathroom.

I tried to correct course, but my coursing anus continued spraying like a muck spreader.

By the time I had positioned myself over the toilet, the evil within my bowels had already been exorcised. Instead of using the toilet as any normal person would have, I had redecorated the entire room.

Drawn towards the door by the emanating smell and my agonized groans, the manager of this fine eating establishment burst into the stall.

As he entered the small room, he witnessed the horrors of the situation:

A six-foot Welsh rugby player holding his trousers and underpants in one hand in a restroom that was now painted brown.

"You get out of my restaurant now, you bad man!" began the irate screaming of this proud restauranteur.

"Flick you, I kill you, you bad man!" was the rantings from the restaurant manager.

"Mate, I am so incredibly sorry," I started to explain. "Please allow me to clean this up and compensate you for this most unfortunate accident."

"You flicking shit in my restaurant, you bad man, I flicking cut off your cock!"

The gentleman could not see the funny side of this poor unfortunate incident, and my attempted amends for my indiscretion went unheard.

"Please allow me to get dressed, and I will help resolve this situation." I said.

"Kim, bring me a knife!" was the order barked from the restaurant owner to the head chef in the nearby kitchen.

"Now let's not be hasty, pal," I tried to say in a patronizing tone.

"You leave now you dirty man, or I flicking kill you!"

At that moment, I thought that all hopes of trying to resolve this with my Welsh charm were fading fast, and so decided to just cut my losses and say farewell before he killed me.

As I tried to pull up my pants, he grabbed my wrist and started to drag me out of the bathroom.

"Hold on, fella. Can I get dressed, please?" I tried to explain.

"Kim...where flicking knife? Bring me now." was again the unreasonable command from this little fella who was now turning red with anger.

Time to leave, I decided and began my walk of shame through the packed restaurant that was full of revelers and holidaymakers.

So, there I was, shorts and underpants in one hand, throbbing knob out for the world to see, and being dragged through the lobby by a small Asian gentleman.

As I was being marched out the front entrance, the background chatter in the room fell silent as all eyes peered upon the guest eviction. However, as I passed by a small table where a couple were sharing a romantic evening meal, I could not pass without saying:

"I would not recommend the fish," as I was thrown onto the street.

With half time over, and the effects of another strong whisky in the blood stream kicking in, we ran back onto the field with a renewed determination to make it through the second half.

The stupidity of event was now evident with most players under running repairs.

There were men with bandages wrapped around heads, ice packs on knees and bodies strapped to stretchers as they were carried from the battlefield. Goldie, in an attempt to inspire a defensive line yelled out:

"Come on lads, stick together."

He looked over at me and we both started to giggle.

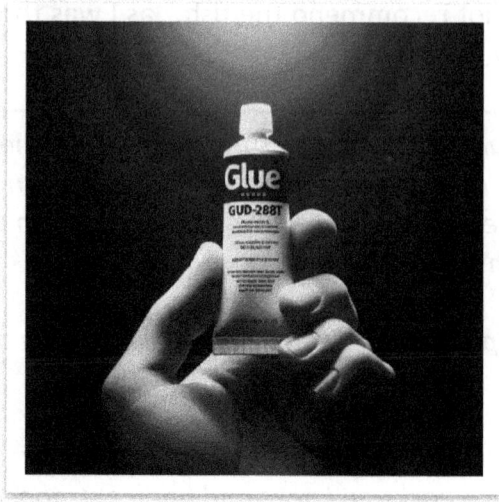

Story 6
Sticky Face

For you unbegun few who have yet to dip your toes into the wild waters of a rugby stag, I implore you to read no further. Spare yourselves these true tales of debauchery.

But for the brave souls among you, you intrepid seekers of mischief and mayhem, strap on your scrum caps and read on.

Ah, the early 2000s: a time of boy bands, of questionable fashion choices, and the birthplace of modern-day Internet pornography. During this bygone era, I had the distinct honour of serving as the best man (or second-best man) for my good friend Goldie.

Goldie, not his real name of course, was a former RAF veteran with a passion for practical jokes and an even greater passion for shooting down the defenses of the fairer sex.

A gentleman rogue armed with an arsenal of outrageous dicky bow ties and a posh English accent that could charm the panties off a Macy's mannequin, Goldie had a knack for leaving a trail of swooning hearts in his wake, each woman falling prey to his mischievous charm.

After pissing away three years at university, Goldie found himself in a peculiar predicament while studying archaeology. He had set his sights on this profession after Steven Spielberg had unleashed the cinematic marvel Jurassic Prank, but realised that to fund his endeavors, he needed a sugar mummy.

Presented with this path, Goldie decided to take the plunge. He resolved to marry a wealthy woman with a penchant for low morals and a high tolerance for inebriates crashing on the sofa.

And so, it was no surprise to his close friends when he announced his decision to marry and that it would be a rather quick affair before the lovely lady had a chance to perform a thorough background check.

With a cunning plan in place, we assembled our intrepid group of twelve rugby disciples, and packed ourselves into a minibus that was held together with hopes and dreams and set forth on what would become an epic journey. Our quest? To conquer not one, not two, but three distinct locations on a stag do for the ages!

We were rugby mates' intent on celebrating the sacred union of one man and one woman in the holy bond of matrimony. However, what unfolded during this celebration defied decency and reason.

With three cities on the itinerary, a lone bus as our trusty steed, a porcelain pig of dubious significance, and a war chest brimming with over 2000 pounds of drinking money, that fateful expedition inflicted on us irreparable emotional and physical scars.

We had planned our journey with reckless abandonment, focusing primarily on where ex-girlfriends were now living in the hope that one or two of them could be encouraged out of retirement to once be charmed into submission.

Our inaugural destination was none other than charming Cheltenham, next stop was Plymouth, and finally Weston Super Mare.

As for Weston Super Mare, it still holds a special place in my heart for a myriad of reasons, not least of which was the fact that it had served as the venue for my own stag and the antics continue to this day as I still have nerve damage in both my thumbs. That story, though, is a tale for another time.

And so, with our first destination firmly set in our GPS and a bus dripping with fuel, we set off on this grand adventure, as we were on a mission from God.

The boys were in high spirits, and we had stocked up on essentials: two party-sized bags of Smith's Cheese and Onion crisps, one packet of ribbed condoms and eight crates of Strongbow. With the open road stretching before us and not a care in the world, we were primed for an unforgettable escapade.

Just over an hour later, we pulled up at the Beehive, which is a popular drinking establishment in the heart of Cheltenham's East. We parked our trusty bus in the car park of the pub and proceeded to get ready ourselves for the night ahead.

As my dim co-conspirators and I swaggered into the even dimmer pub, the air was throbbing with anticipation. Poor Goldie, our unsuspecting friend, began to second-guess his choice of companions, wondering if he'd somehow stumbled into horror move as a half pint of spirits was ordered and a cider chaser, just to get us going. His left eye twitched, and the colour drained from his face as he contemplated the gravity of choosing this bunch of friends to take charge of his bachelor party.

But the relentless cheers persisted, and Goldie knew he had no choice but to enjoy the night. With a resigned sigh, he embraced the challenge, first swallowing the half pint in one audacious gulp, followed by the cider to drown out the fiery taste.

The ravelment had begun, and as we sat there the pre-arranged entertainment started to arrive at the fine establishment. Twenty two ladies from Goldie's past had been invited to the soiree and they were intent on showing their gratitude for past experiences, although three of them were currently very pregnant.

As the brave stag tourists began to buzz around the Beehive pub that following morning, they resembled a crew of hungover Hyperboreans preparing to raid the next town on our itinerary.

Following a quick head count it was revealed that a couple of the stag soldiers were absent, potentially abducted by some of the ex-girlfriends who had lured the men them away with scandalous promises of Narnian Turkish delights. Yet our valiant mission was to march our dear stag down the aisle, and we expected this treacherous journey would take casualties.

With our mission still at hand, we clambered into our trusty steed once more and departed Cheltenham, headed west on the A4, our numbers now reduced but our quest for the Holy Grail of lasting matrimony still firmly fixed in our minds.

We recalibrated our provisions, and each reveller found themselves blessed with three-quarters of a cider case instead of a mere half. The logic was clear: fewer pit stops to replenish our liquid courage on the three-hour voyage ahead, avoidance of rabbits with vicious streaks and only the potential for a couple of bladder breaks and the purchasing of a small shrubbery, in case we bumped into the knight who say 'Knee'.

As we approached the M3 Motorway, a glimmer of hope pierced the haze of our hangovers. Lo and behold, the missing duo of lost warriors were stumbling along in the same direction as our dilapidated bus! Thunderous applause and a chorus of horns greeted them as we pulled over.

"Where in the world have you been?" echoed the cries from the back of the bus.

"There's no leaving the tour! Pray, what's your excuse?" demanded the stag party.

"Two sisters were up for a foursome," came the unabashed reply.

"Well, that's four excuses!"

The bus doors closed, sealing our fate. The saga of the previous night's escapades was demanded without omitting a single sordid detail.

And so, our bellies full of beer again, the grand tour continued.

The journey from Cheltenham to Plymouth, a mere one hundred and fifty miles, or about two hundred and forty kilometers for those who have embraced the metric system, of English adventure — a three-hour drive if the traffic cooperates, but in Britain, distance and time are like squabbling siblings who can't agree on anything, not unlike the royal family.

Motoring in the UK is challenging at the best of times, but once you venture past Exeter, the last bastion of civilization, you enter *The Twilight Zone.*

Sheep playing chicken with your car, cows conducting road rallies, tractors making impromptu appearances, and horses strutting their stuff. And let's not forget the never-ending roadworks—because, clearly, the UK has an annual quota to meet when it comes to traffic cones.

So, what's a group of intrepid travelers to do to pass the time? Well, Rugby drinking games, of course.

"Spoof" is a game of cunning and deception, and "drink while you think" is an excuse to sip your beverage while pondering the mysteries of the universe—or the traffic ahead.

Spoof

> *This sport of kings is played by any number of degenerates. In each round, the objective is to guess the aggregate number of coins concealed*

by all the players, with each player allowed to smuggle up to three coins in his hand.

At the beginning of every round, each player conceals several coins, or no coins at all, in their closed fist, extended into the circle of play. The initial player calls what they think is the total number of coins. Play proceeds clockwise around the circle until each player has ventured a call regarding the total number of coins, and no player can call the same total as any other player otherwise they could be ejected from the bus!

After all players have made their calls, they open their fists and display their coins for the group to tally up the total. If no player guesses the right total, the entire group continues to play in the next round.

Play continues until all players have been eliminated except for one, whereupon that last man standing pays the stipulated stakes, which can be as outrageous as the group deems appropriate to each other player, which usually means finishing whatever drink they have in their hand but can be as dastardly as losing an eyebrow.

Drink while you think

This drinking game is based on naming famous people and focuses on the first letter of the famous person's last name. For instance, if the first name is Michael Jordan, then the next person chugs their beer until they think of a famous person whose first name begins with 'J', like 'James Franco'. Names cannot be repeated, so the longer the game lasts, the harder it gets, and the more alcohol is quaffed. But on a rugby trip, the famous person can be substituted for absolutely anything, including names of front row players, sexual positions not covered in the Kama Sutra, or even more risky topics like ex-girlfriends who have interesting tattoos in strange places on their bodies.

After what seemed like an eternity, we veered off the A38 and steered our wayward carriage of revelry towards the enchanting Sutton Harbor, where our accommodation for the evening had been booked.

Expecting resistance to a rugby group booking, we had cunningly phoned ahead and acquired the necessary rooms for the evening under the ingenious alias of the "Oxford Old-Boys Chess Team."

Now, imagine the poor innkeeper's face when we pulled up in our sorry excuse for a bus, which by this point was hissing and steaming like a temperamental tea kettle, all thanks to the sheer weight of the lads crammed into the back. With an air of casual nonchalance, we sauntered in and announced our arrival, or rather, our grand entrance.

"A baker's dozen of beers, my good sir!" we declared, as though we'd just crossed the Sahara and were in dire need of liquid sustenance to quench our epic thirst.

The landlord's surprise must have been something to behold, as he realized that chess teams, even Oxford Old-Boys ones, don't typically roll in like a rowdy gang of beer-thirsty pirates.

After dropping off our bags, we headed out into the night, on a quest for the finest ale, convivial company, and perhaps the promise of a curry to cap off the evening with a tale or two of our misadventures. But what transpired next caught me utterly off guard.

The night had started off in a reasonably good manner, with a few cheeky ales, a wink from a barmaid which had the potential to turn into something later on that night and a seedy night club that was strategically positioned next to several Goldie and chip shops.

"Dear sirs," announced our beloved stag, "It's been a splendid pleasure, but I find myself weary and in dire need of slumber."

"Dear Goldie, you're having a laugh!" I sputtered, flabbergasted.

"I bid you all adieu."

Goldie left us behind to continue our merry escapades, and headed off back to the hotel for what he thought was going to be a nice evening in.

And there I sat, thunderstruck. Just as the evening was hitting its stride, my charge decided it was time for a cup of tea and a cosy night's sleep.

"No... no, no, no, no, no, no!" I stammered. "No, no, no, no bloody way!"

Only I and the Norse God Loki understood the cosmic malevolence that was about to be unleashed.

"If he wants to act like a chicken, then by Jove, a chicken he shall be," we agreed.

Moments after Goldie swam out of the pub, I broke the news to the rest of the stag party about his heinous betrayal and outlined the provisions needed for our retaliatory plan.

"Right, lads," I began, a sinister glint in my eye. "Here's what I need each of you to find:

"Gweebo, you get some golden Syrup,"

"Little Elvis, go find a pair of washing up glove."

"Hedgehog, hair removal cream."

"Where the hell do I I get that from?"

"Try Boots, the chemists, and get four tubes, he's a hairy bugger."

"Buster, go with Hedgehog and get some food colouring, preferably pink."

"Lee, a feather pillow."

"And I'll find some super glue."

Each member of our merry band was tasked with acquiring one item, and we were to rendezvous at the hotel by four o'clock in the morning at the very latest or else be presumed dead.

As the hour of reckoning drew near, the lads assembled outside the guesthouse, their faces beaming with delight that the elusive items had been secured. To our collective surprise, a couple of pairs of ladies' undergarments had also somehow made their way into our stash.

"What in the bloody hell are you planning to do with these?" came the curious inquiry.

"If he wants to be a chicken, then a chicken he shall be! Lads, our mission is a good old-fashioned tar and feathering!"

Now, try to imagine poor Goldie's astonishment when a dozen hulking figures barged into his pre-dawn bedroom. In the blink of an eye, the bed covers were flung aside, and he found himself pinned to the bed.

Every stitch of clothing was summarily removed, and two entire tubes of hair removal cream were slathered all over his hapless body.

The instructions had been explicit on the tube of hair removal cream: no more than seven minutes between application and removal. Yet, somehow, twenty excruciating minutes later, with the scent of singed flesh wafting through the air, finally Goldie was rinsed clean.

He emerged from the ordeal looking like a newborn babe, naked and hairless from neck to toe, save for the mop on his head.

"Don't you look lovely?" one of the lads muttered from the back of the room.

"Pass me the pink food dye, please," I instructed.

"Ugg urr," Goldie tried to speak from beneath the weight of lads lying on top of him.

"What's that?"

"Up yours," Goldie muttered before being restrained once again and then gagged for good measure.

In seconds, Goldie transformed from a pale, sobbing infant into a shade of red that rivalled the sun's core. Then came the treacly goo, smeared liberally across his rosy skin, followed by the strategic pillow rupture, releasing a flurry of feathers that alighted on the poor stag's naked, reddened, and blistering skin.

Now, in all honesty, I should have called it a day at that point, but there was the matter of the super glue which had been on sale and I bought the value pack to save money, so didn't want it to go to waste. As I prepared to smear the sticky substance onto the washing gloves, ready to adhere it to Goldie's nether regions, I should have realized that this might just be a tad too much for him to bear.

With the glue-laden glove in one hand and the rest of the adhesive in the other, I advanced upon Goldie, cackling with malevolent glee.

Summoning his inner chicken, Goldie broke free and snatched the glove from my hand, sending glue splattering all around the room, but mostly in my eyes.

My immediate reaction was to wipe the sticky mess from my face with my one free hand, but alas, my reflexes weren't swift enough, and due to its rapid hardening characteristics, I found myself with my right index finger firmly attached to my own eye!

And at that juncture, the landlord had reached the limits of his patience. He could no longer entertain the notion that we were a Chess Club.

Bursting into the room, he yelled out "You're not the Oxford Old-Boys!"

Greeted by the sight of a dozen inebriated men, the pungent scent of singed man-flesh, feathers strewn about like confetti, a disgruntled human chicken, and a man with his finger stuck to his own face with what looked like a thick creamy liquid.

Not my finest hour, but then again, what do you expect when you bring superglue to a stag party?

With the basic skills of passing the ball proving more difficult due to fatigue, and the fact that our water bottles had been substituted for whisky, there was an increase in the number of handling errors.

This meant that there were more opportunities for scrums.

A rugby union scrum for those of you not accustomed to its purpose, is a chaotic spectacle of brute force, to restart the game when there is a knock on in play. This involves eight players locking their heads and shoulders together and pushing against one another. I took my position in the front row and readied myself for the shoving.

"How hard do you want me to push"? came the question from Buster in the second row.

"As hard as I pushed on you in Paris" I replied.

For the second time that afternoon, Buster froze.

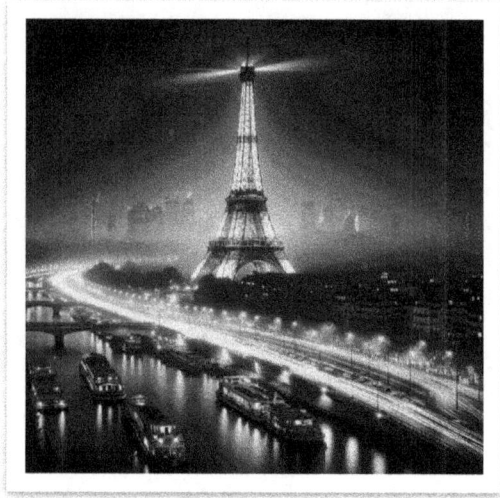

Story 7

Misadventures in Paris

Set in the early 1990s, before the widespread use of mobile phones, Instagram, and political correctness, my Cardiff University Rugby Team and I decided to go to Paris for the Wales v France Rugby match at Parc des Princes - the French stronghold of brutal forward power and scintillating back-line attacking play.

The only drawback to this cracking plan was money: the exorbitant cost of accommodation in the city of love, the English Channel, and the means to travel 750 km with less than 20 pounds for each man on tour. It was a challenge, but where there was a will, there was a way. Hence, a call to the Cardiff University President with the promise of cultural harmony and relationship building between two great universities: ours and the Paris Université Club (PUC).

You see, the Cardiff University Social President at that time was one Yasseme Homé, a wonderful man in his own right, but desperate to leave his mark by fostering good relationships beyond the boundaries of South Wales. Hence, in his divine wisdom, he assumed that matching 28 Welsh University Rugby players, hell-bent on a drunken and debaucherous weekend away in Paris, with a similarly named institute of learning was a good thing. He did not know that at that time PUC was one of the strongest rugby teams in the French premier rugby scene, boasting 5 full international rugby players and 7 emerging talents, who would go on to dominate the world of rugby over the next decade.

In comparison, we had five fairly decent players, fifteen lads up for a drunken weekend, a 22-stone Scottish winger nicknamed Jock, and eight associate friends who thought they were just getting a lift to London to see family members for the weekend.

As we left the University on that fateful Thursday afternoon on a bus creaking under the weight of Welsh beef and Strongbow cider, poor Yasseme must have thought he had taken his first step on the road towards a Nobel Peace Prize for diplomatic relationships. He thought he could achieve what no one before him could - friendship and harmony between the English and French, at last. How wrong he was! Very wrong indeed.

With several hours available to drive the 228 km to the port of Dover, via the southern side of the M25, we assumed we had plenty of time. Then it would be just a short ferry crossing over to France, and then the remaining 500 km towards the Paris Université Club at Pierre de Coubertin.

What we hadn't considered, though, was that our dear bus, laden with a quarter of a tonne of men and another 100 kilograms of beer, could only break the 70-mile-an-hour speed limit on the motorway on the rare occasion that the road was clear and on a downward gradient. This meant that to make the trip in four hours, there were absolutely no stopping breaks, not even for the toilet.

For my dear friend Buster, who was already into his third can of Strongbow, this was going to mean pain and suffering, the likes of which would bring tears of laughter and amusement to those of us who could calculate bladder volume against distance to travel.

We arrived at the port six hours after setting off from Cardiff, just in time for the last ferry of the evening and took our position in the queue. As we came to a slow stop behind the long row of cars in front of us, the low whimpering sound from Buster's discomfort and need to release himself was reaching a climax as he tried to hold in his pee.

During the journey, as we had passed through Kent, with some 60 km still to go before arriving at the port of Dover, poor Buster had begun to complain that not only was his bladder completely full, but his kidneys were also beginning to hurt as the excessive liquid began backing up his ureters, impeding his bodily functions.

Of course, no sympathy had been offered. So, when the bus finally came to a stop at the port, a clammy-looking Buster stumbled from the bus, clutching his stomach. He hastily unbuttoned his trousers and, with great relief, began to release the half gallon of water he now had sloshing around on his insides. He was oblivious to the children in the opposite car, who were looking with horror as a crying man began to urinate on the ground. If the Guinness Book of Records had been there, it would have resulted in a new category being created, entitled 'longest wee by a male'.

The ferry ride was uneventful, with only the odd mishap as some of the boys tried to score a date with a French lady heading back to Paris. But overall, the majority of the team had taken the opportunity to get some sleep.

The next morning, as we arrived in Calais, the sun was rising, and a renewed hope of a win on foreign soil beckoned the lads, alongside the promise of tales from the red-light district in the Pigalle District and the high kicking shenanigans of the Moulin Rouge.

As our trusty bus, now smelling a little fusty, continued its merry way towards our destination, attention turned to the upcoming match between us and the Paris Université Club.

In our team of happy travellers, we did not have the superior attacking skills to mount a strong backline attack, nor did we have the strategic movement of a fast and athletic lineout.

We, therefore, decided that we would lure them into a false sense of security during the first half of the game, and then surprise them in the last 30 minutes.

Settled on this strategic intent, we backed it up by the tactical decision that all members of the starting 15 would consume one bottle of red wine each, and a pint of peeled prawns before kick-off!

We arrived at our accommodation just at the outskirts of Paris. Obviously, we had not expected five-star accommodation with canapés on arrival and fine champagne, but a communal dorm with bunk beds three levels high was not quite what we had expected either for the discounted rate of 5 euros per night.

With the expectation that all of us would be going home with French models after the rugby game, beguiled by the Welsh charm and Casanova-like pick-up lines, we settled in and started to get changed for the upcoming game.

We were in high spirits as we arrived at the rugby ground, but they were soon dulled by the fact that around 10,000 PUC supporters were making their way to the Stade Charléty ahead of us.

As we stepped off our bus, a foreboding feeling fell over us of what was to come. However, it was too late for any possibility of professionalism as the wine had already been drunk and the bus was reeking of fresh Goldie and seafood dressing.

As we stepped off the bus to make our way to the changing rooms, we were presented with the game day programme. They had us down as Cardiff Rugby Union, which at the time, was a premier grade rugby team, boasting 12 Welsh international players on its books, unlike Cardiff University Rugby Team, which boasted 12 players who were not yet totally pissed.

Nevertheless, we took the field and gave our best, eventually going down 96-3 after a heroic last 10 minutes where we held the score line to under 100 points. Additionally, we managed to milk a penalty after working an amazing back-of-the-lineout move with a switch back to the blind side, which released our 21-stone Scottish winger into space with 20 metres to go to the PUC try line.

He nearly made it, but before he could score the try, he was viciously tackled by the imposing up-and-coming Wallabies International prop, Roo, which left poor Jock sprawled out on the pitch, clutching his jawbone, now slightly dislodged after the handiwork of Roo.

With the game over, and the body parts retrieved from the field, we managed to make our way to the PUC clubhouse, where a fine meal and some beers had been put on for us.

We apologized for our poor performance, and swore vengeance against our University President Yasseme Homé, who had arranged the fixture not knowing the mismatch in standards between the two universities.

However, as with all rugby matches, friendships were made, relationships were built, and soon, we were all heading off into the Paris evening to experience the highs and lows of Parisian nightlife.

As we made our way from drinking establishment to drinking establishment, the je ne sais quoi of Paris was undeniable. The sounds, smells, and sheer spectacle of the city were amazing. We made our way to the Trocadéro, the site of Palais de Chaillot, which overlooks the Eiffel Tower, and where a priest was handing out leaflets encouraging lost rugby souls towards the way of light and God.

The priest asked me if I would like one of his leaflets and so, not to be rude, and after believing that somehow I had miraculously learned to speak French in the last 24 hours, I replied: "Non merci, je suis une pomme de terre." Which roughly translates as no thank you, I'm a potato!

As we moved through the city, taking in the Avenue des Champs-Élysées and the beautiful Seine river, before staggering our way back to the Stade Charléty, some 15 kilometres south of the city, we miraculously came across a random wheelbarrow, left by the god of drunken rugby men, into which we bundled the exhausted Jock, before Buster, Scooter and I wheeled him safe and sound back to our dorm room accommodation, as the dawn ascended.

The four of us came crashing into the dorm, which was smelling rancid with the scent of beer, farts, cigarettes, and cheap wine, and duly made our way up to the top bunks, which were the only ones left unoccupied.

At this point, I must admit I was tired, after having walked the ridiculous 15 km home, pushing a 21-stone man in a wheelbarrow, but when Buster decided to start singing and pretending to crow like a French cockerel, I did offer a kind suggestion that he settle down and go to sleep.

Unfortunately, he didn't, and shortly afterwards, my tolerance for his antics reached rock bottom.

In my mind, a final warning had already been issued, so when the relentless and hairy Wookie once again started singing, he should have known that a response was coming.

As I sprang over the three bunk beds that separated me from Buster, a few factors unfolded. Firstly, it was still dark, and I could not distinguish him from the shadows of the room. Secondly, I was unaware that Buster was used to sleeping naked and had already removed all his clothes. And finally, he was face down as he tried to get under the bed sheets.

As I cleared the remaining bed, ready to give him a playful, but direct punch to what I thought would be his chest, I unfortunately landed on him with my right index finger lodged squarely up his ass!

From the dead of the night, the emancipated Buster let out the high-pitched squeal:

"Oww, that's inside!" and silence fell about the room.

As I strode back across the bunk beds, fear had descended upon the room. The goal of quietness had indeed been achieved but at a high cost of the personal dignity of my dear friend, who went on to become the God Father to my youngest son. From there on, my best friend had become my Paris Bitch.

In contrast, the return trip to Cardiff was very subdued. Battered, bruised, and violated, we chugged our way back to South Wales, and the Students Union Bus depot, and the engine on the bus had finally given in.

We bid each other goodbye, as we slowly made our way back to our respective student accommodation, but a bond was made that trip between two heterosexual men that will never be broken. A bond of friendship, shared experience, and a story to be re-told at any opportunity.

The game continued, and as the clock slowly crept towards full time, we had a lineout on the halfway line.

Scooter threw the ball in, which instead of being caught, bounced of Buster's head and landed back into his own arms.
Seizing the opportunity, he headed off down the sideline and went crashing over the try line to score.

As he walked back to the halfway line he called out:

"That was unexpected."

"Indeed," I replied, "Just like that time we ended up in Helsinki."

Story 8

Helsinki

In the heart of England, just north of London, lies a quaint little village named Waltham Abbey. An idyllic place with a communal green, a church and a couple of old-fashioned pubs. If you were to visit, you would say that it was a cozy and tranquil location where nothing out of the ordinary happens apart from local gossip and the occasional swingers party.

That was of course until I decided to call in on my good mate Scooter. It all started with an innocent arrangement to catch up for a few pints, some laughs, and some reminiscent of past escapades. Little did we suspect that destiny had a different plan for us that weekend, which would test our bank accounts and sanity.

It had been a few years since Scooter and I had last caught up, which was when we had taken the field together for an exhibition rugby match in Devon. It had been a great afternoon with some strong scrummaging followed by the re-kindling of a few drinking games and some new friendships made.

I had just returned from an overseas business trip to Atlanta, Georgia, and had landed at Heathrow Airport, which is on the West side of London. I had fought through the Friday grid of the M25 motorway and the torrential English rain arriving at Waltham Abbey midafternoon tired, but thirsty for a few beers.

I parked my car outside Scooter's home, and I knocked on the door.

Now there is something about friendship between men that women just don't get, and that's the ability to turn up on a mate's doorstep, hurl abuse at him, and expect the same banter in return. To an outsider it might seem odd, but when you have played rugby together, shedding blood and sweat for each other; well, it's just the way things are.

I knocked on the door, and a few moments later Scooter answered.

"How you doing ass face?"

"Ha ha... you old wanker, you look fat."

"Not as fat as your mother!"

"You staying the night?"

"Yes please, mate."

"No worries, fancy a few pints down the pub?"

"Go on then, but just one or two."

With pleasantries exchanged and the spirit of adventure brewing, we set out for the nearest pub, The Three Bells, a rustic establishment with fine ale and a dart board, blissfully unaware that we would soon be departing for more exotic locations.

We merrily skipped the two hundred meters or so from Scooter's home to the local pub, and as we waltzed in, a couple of pints were summoned forth, accompanied by an order of chips for sustenance.

With beer flowing and memories pouring, we found ourselves reflecting on the yawning gap since our last escapade – a whopping three years had passed since the exhibition rugby game in Devon!

Just as we were about to toast to the good old days, the barman waltzed over with an extra round of pints and two shots of black sambuca. Fate, it seemed, had decided to intervene, and kick this reunion up a notch.

With the added alcohol, and the lowering of inhibitions, the conversation turned to the atrocious weather.

"It's been bloody raining for weeks," Scooter exclaimed.

"I've been stuck in the house for the last three weekends."

"Do you know where the weather is always great?" I replied.

"Ibiza, they have three hundred days of sun every year, and the beer is only one pound a bottle."

"Then what the hell are we doing here? We should catch a flight to the sun and make a weekend of this catch up."

We both took a sip from our beer and pondered as to the insanity of this impromptu trip suggestion.

"Well," I began, "I do have my passport, and you look like you could do with some sun you pale faced twat."

After a bit more encouragement from the other chaps in the pub and a few more pints, the decision to take a last-minute flight to Ibiza was a go.

With a long weekend ahead in the UK, the plan was to jet off on that very Friday night and return late on Sunday seemed a great reasonable approach, leaving Monday for recovery before heading back to work on Tuesday.

Scooter picked up the phone and called his wife.

"Hello love, how's your day been?"

"Good, good, that's nice. Can you do me a small favour, please?"

There was a pause as the pub listened in on the high-pitched yelling that was now coming down the phone from Scooter wife.

"Yes, love…. Yes… you are right. Yes, love, just put that on the list of things to do and I will do that as well."

There seemed to be a long list of jobs that were being added to Scooters' tasks for that weekend. After what seemed like a good five minutes of instructions, there was a pause.

"Can you bring my passport down the pub, please? I'm going to Ibiza this weekend with Milo."

Now, it's crucial to understand that hindsight is a wonderful thing. The pub banter was electric, the beer was flowing, plus the Rugby World Cup was on. By the time the clock struck 9:00 PM and there had been no sign of Scooter's wife, we thought that the trip was off. But then, just when we were contemplating calling it a night, heading for a curry at the local Indian restaurant and then heading home, a very angry looking lady walked into the pub, threw Scooters passport at him, and yelled:

"I'm off to my mother's, do what the hell you want this weekend."

Cheers erupted around the pub, loud clapping and whistling engulfed the air, and a malevolent smile crept across the face of destiny.

With Scooter's wife off to see her dear mother, we had no idea how we were now going to get to Stanstead airport, which was on the Northeast of London, but only about fifteen miles from where we currently were.

A drunken phone call was made.

How we managed to convince Scooter's mother to be our chauffeur that fateful evening remains a mystery only the gods might unravel. Nevertheless, she dropped us off at the Airport, where we rolled out of the car, bid adieu to her, and staggered into the terminal with the grace of slightly inebriated schoolgirls.

The ticketing desk became our first hurdle, and we posed the all-important question to the lady who was about to clock off for the evening:

"Excuse us, Miss, when does the next flight to Ibiza depart?"

Horrified to learn that there were no more flights that evening, our intoxicated dreams were paused, however, we were equipped with a sense of adventure that was undeniable and instantly remembered the immortal words of Clint Eastwood in the classic nineties' movie *Heartbreak Ridge*, and so we adapted, improvised and overcame.

Not willing to return home with our tails between our legs, we opted instead to book into a local hotel so that we could come back to the airport that following morning and renew our adventure. After a frantic search through the phone directory, we found a suitable accommodation only eighteen miles away which had one room left for the evening– the honeymoon suite.

Arriving at the hotel close to midnight, the manager at the reception desk shot us a peculiar look as we forked over two hundred and fifty pounds for a night in the lover's suite. She couldn't resist a sly wink and a whispered promise of freshly changed sheets for our special evening ahead.

Instead of setting the record straight, we played along. I patted Scooter on the bottom and loudly declared:

"A little experimentation wouldn't hurt," and the landlady let out a giggle.

The honeymoon suite unfolded before us – a grand four-poster bed, a king-sized bathroom, and a basket of fruit for added romance. Some fresh towels and 'His and Hers' robes were draped on the edge of the bed.

Has the realisation of the situation dawned upon us, in that the hotel we were hold up in for the night was three miles further from the airport than from where we had started that evening, Scooter had decided that enough was enough, and it was time for bed.

Being a fine heterosexual man, he jumped into bed fully clothed and was asleep within seconds, followed, a few moments later, by ear splitting snoring.

As he was already in dreamland, thinking about golden beaches and scantily clad ladies on the beaches of Ibiza, I thought that there was just one last opportunity for a prank.

I slowly retrieved Scooter credit card from his wallet and turned on the TV.

I navigated to the 'pay per view' menu on the screen and selected the adult channels. Faced with the option of one movie for nine ninety-nine, or all channels including erotic male gay porn for thirty-nine ninety-nine I chose the latter.

I completed the registration process by giving over Scooters credit card details before I too drifted off to sleep, giggling at what explanation he would have to give to his wife when she checked the bill at the end of the month.

The next morning arrived, and armed with a faint hangover, we rose early. After indulging in a hearty meal from the obligatory breakfast buffet, where our every move was scrutinized under the judgmental gaze of other hotel manager, we once again embarked on our journey to the airport, ready to conquer the Mediterranean.

Back at the airport once more, with renewed excitement of the impending adventure we thought we would inject an extra dose of mystery and a sense of "who dares wins" into our escapade, we decided to book a flight without knowing our exact destination as there were many fine Mediterranean destinations serviced by Stanstead Airport.

Approaching the ticket desk with a devil-may-care attitude, I said:

"Two tickets on the next available flight, please."

The customer services lady looked at me with a mix of confusion and concern as I added:

"Make it somewhere unique."

"Do you want to know the destination?" she asked cautiously.

"No, that way it'll be a surprise," thereby, sealing our fate.

With a swipe of the credit card, we were locked in and ready to get underway.

"Have a good flight, and good luck."

So, there we were at the airport, 8:30 AM in the morning, tickets in hand, and a sense of anticipation in our step. Seated at the bar, Scooter had already secured a couple of pints. As I pulled up a seat next to him, he asked,

"Where are we going?"

"I have no idea," I chuckled. "It's an adventure."

It dawned on us at that moment that we had sauntered into the airport with no luggage, no change of clothes, only the clothes we had on and a passport. In our assumption that we were bound for the winter sun of the Mediterranean, we hadn't thought beyond what we were wearing.

With a twinge of trepidation, I opened the tickets and discovered that, instead of heading south to an exotic destination, we were bound for a place called Helsinki.

"Where is Helsinki?" I asked Scooter.

"I think it's one of the Greek Islands," he quipped.

"Let me grab a Lonely Planet guidebook and check," he added, returning a few minutes later with a book he had purchased from the news agent inside the departure hall, and an amused glint in his eye.

As he perused the guidebook, giggles erupted, and tears started to stream down his face.

It turned out that Helsinki was darker and colder than the UK during the months of November through to February, with average temperatures hovering around zero degrees Celsius.

Undeterred, Scooter revealed two fluorescent orange balaclavas with eye and mouth holes, declaring that we'd be fine if we limited our exposure to the northern Arctic winds to no more than fifteen minutes at a time.

Boarding the plane armed with nothing but a small rain jacket and our vibrant orange balaclavas, we took our seats at the back of the plane amidst passengers decked out in Arctic survival gear.

"Can I check your ticket one more time, please?" a concerned Cabin Crew member asked.

"And you are aware you are on a plane to Finland, Sir?"

"We sure are." I replied with a smile on my face.

"And what may I ask are the balaclavas for?"

"Well, that's in case we get cold. Plus, the Polar Bears will see us coming."

The logic was undeniable, and so the Cabin Crew lady handed us back our tickets and made a quick call to the cockpit to inform the Flight Crew that there was no cause for concern, we were just rugby players on a jolly weekend away.

And so, in a blaze of orange, we soared into the unknown, armed with courage, laughter, and the undeniable truth that sometimes, the best adventures are the ones you stumble into, half-cocked and wholly unprepared.

Our misadventures continued as our flight, already delayed by the whims of unruly weather, finally managed to land at 9:00 PM in the evening. Our destination, the illustrious city of Helsinki had been experiencing an Arctic Blizzard!

During our extended stay at the airport, trapped in the clutches of weather-induced limbo, we exhibited the rare foresight to book ahead and had secured a four-star hotel smack dab in the heart of the city.

As we stumbled into our hotel, with balaclavas pulled down and steam coming from our breath, the check in receptionist looked up from the desk in utter bewilderment.

"Can I help you Sirs?"

"Reservation under the name of Scooter please."

"Certainly Sir. Ah yes, I have you here in the system. One night in the luxury suite. And how will you be paying for that?"

Since I had booked the flights, Scooter had agreed to pick up the hotel bill.

"And are you okay if I hold one hundred pounds on the credit card just in case you want to purchase any extras?"

"Sure, no problem."

Little did Scooter know that there were already 'extras' on his bank statement.

As we entered our room, Scooter shot off to the bathroom to wash off the travel grime with a quick shower before we headed off into Helsinki for the night.

Seizing the opportunistic moment to continue the credit card prank, I flicked on the TV and quickly navigated to the adult porn channels.

This collection seemed a little more adventurous than the one Scooter had unknowingly purchased in the UK, but again there was a special on for the purchase of a packaged bundle which was just too good a deal to pass up.

With the selection of titles such as 'Scooby Do does her again' and 'Naughty teacher, naught pupil' picked, I turned off the brightness of the screen all the way down so that Scooter would not be able to see what was playing on the screen.

Now comfortably arrived in the city of Helsinki, and armed with our trusty orange balaclavas, we braved the frosty Finnish night and waltzed into the city's main drinking establishments with all the subtlety of a bull in a China shop. The risk of frostbite and the indignant stares of the locals were mere trifles as we crashed through the door of the first pub in our path.

Now, it's a universal enigma as to why there is an Irish bar in every corner of the globe, but that evening, we were overjoyed to stumble upon O'Malley's Tavern.

As we burst through the doors of the pub on that cold Helsinki night, the barman seemed shocked to see two chaps dressed in orange balaclavas saunter up to the bar and casually say.

"Two pints of ale, please."

Following a short pause, in which he tried to work out if this was a robbery or not, Scooter added:

"Mate, you haven't seen any Polar Bears have you?"

His demeanor turned from concern to amusement.

"Nope, just cougars."

And he nodded towards a group of twenty or so females on the other side of the pub who were having a jolly old time.

"Who are they?"

"They are the national Finish Women's Rugby Team."

"Excellent !" Scooter chimed in.

"Send over two dozen black sambucas and say it's from the two elite English scrummaging coaches standing at the bar."

"You are from England?" the barman asked.

"He is, but I'm from Wales." I interjected.

"That explains everything."

And so that's how we ended up in Helsinki teaching the Finish Women's Rugby Team how to scrummage.

We staggered back to our hotel a mere forty-five minutes before we had to leave for the airport to catch the 6:00 AM flight back to Stanstead.

Scooter, perhaps in a semi-hungover haze, cast a cursory glance at his hotel bill and said nothing. Clearly, he had not seen the small fortune that had been charged to his credit card with slightly risqué movie titles that had sneakily found their way onto his tab.

Undeterred by our late-night escapades, we shuffled back to the airport, boarded the flight with no further mishaps or side adventures, and nodded off into slumber, wondering what the devil had just happened.

Such is the stuff of legends, spontaneous journeys, impromptu scrummaging training, and a trail of unexpected charges left behind like breadcrumbs of mischievous mirth.

And so, with our heads full of memories and our wallets slightly lighter, we soared back to the UK, leaving Helsinki with a tale to tell.

But the sweetest cherry on top? Scooter's valiant attempts to convince his wife that the added charges to his hotel bill were the result of a clerical error. Oh, the audacity.

> *With the game over, and no major injuries requiring immediate hospitalisation, relief spread across the team. We returned to the changing rooms where the beer had been pored and the jovial banter of post-match camaraderie was in full swing.*
>
> *We showered, bandaged our open wounds, administered ice packs to our swollen limbs and discussed which pub would be best to head to for the evening.*
>
> *There were many fine pubs to consider, but none better than the Tivoli.*

Story 9

The Tivoli

Unfortunately, The Tivoli is but a memory now, having met its demise in the early 2000s when it was torn down to make room for an upscale wine bar. Before its destruction though it played host to the most outrageous of stag venues.

During my time at university, I enjoyed not only lifelong friendships sun from the rugby field but also through my engineering studies, and amongst those academic giants there emerged a chap destined for greatness in the world of Mechanical construction.

Let's call him the BFG—Big Friendly Genius—for the sake of preserving his not-so-innocent anonymity. A man of great intellect who completed his degree, master's, and doctorate in the space of only seven years.

Following the completion of his studies, BFG decided to take the immediate plunge into marital bliss and had decided to wed his most beloved girlfriend who was clearly far too good looking for him.

Having introduced the two of them a couple of years previously during a summer rugby ball, I received an invitation to his stag party which promised to be a very sophisticated affair, orchestrated not by the BFG himself but by his best man—a rising star in the legal realms of West Wales.

BFG wasn't exactly thrilled about the prospect of a civilized celebration as after seven years of perpetual learning, studying the riveting subject of Tribology – a fancy terms for the science of lubrication, he was ready to let loose and experience carnal pleasures.

After extensive deliberation and sound counsel, a brilliant plan was hatched. The best man during the actual wedding day would be his legal eagle friend, ensuring the wedding day would indeed be a sophisticated affair. But, for the stag do—oh, that was my domain. I was entrusted with the noble task of orchestrating a night so legendary that it could rival Guy Fawkes' ill-fated political celebration at the Houses of Parliament.

Having formed a strong friendship with BFG during my time in University, I wanted to give him a sendoff that would be remembered for years to come. So, in the pursuit of maximum effectiveness and a healthy dose of debauchery, a strategic reconnaissance mission was in order.

The first hurdle was to pinpoint the country, city, and pub that would serve as the venue for an epic night of adventure, and as luck would have it, and without much contemplation there was only one option on the table— The Tivoli.

It had everything that we needed. A bar stocked with fine ale, a room to play snooker in, a barbeque area on the odd occasion the British weather allowed for an outside meal, but most importantly it was run by my dear friend named Rude Dog who was a functioning alcoholic and who owed me several favors.

Adding to my excitement, and as part of my conditional acceptance as 'Stag Best Man' I had insisted that there were absolutely zero restrictions on my stag night planning which included the need for a reconnaissance mission to the Tivoli.

Arriving at ground zero, I took a seat at the bar, and a pint of beer magically appeared before me curtesy of Rude Dog. I started to explain the upcoming mission, and deep negotiations commenced on how this pub could be transformed into the ultimate stag do haven.

"So, you want to have a few beers?" Rude Dog inquired.

"Yes, about two hundred."

"Excellent, and spirits?" the negotiations were going in the right direction.

"Top shelf spirits, and some nasty port should be fine."

"Very good choice." The excitement was growing in the bar man friend.

"And food?" he continued.

"Chips and pies for thirty blokes should be adequate."

"And entertainment?" The look for devilment filled Rude Dog's mind.

"That my friend, I leave up to you."

After a few more beers and some haggling over the ingenious use of the snooker room as suitable to hold a kangaroo court in, a deal was struck. For the princely sum of twenty-two pounds, the venue was secured, entertainment locked in, and Rude Dog himself promised to whip up the culinary delights.

In hindsight, I probably should have grilled the Rude Dog for more details, but the twinkle in his eye hinted that the less I knew, the bigger the surprise. And hey, Rude Dog had never let me down before, so I felt confident that everything was falling into place.

Oh, how wrong I was.

In the days leading up to the weekend of the tour, I phoned the other members of the stag party to collect tales of mischief about the BFG.

Every single one of them had a story to share about his past indiscretions. So much so that we decided to hold a kangaroo court where he would be held to account for his crimes.

So many stories of darkness were revealed; a cascade of crimes that would make even seasoned miscreant's blush. Plenty of material for any kangaroo court, and so a guaranteed guilty verdict was in the bag even before the first charge was read out.

As we rolled up to the Tivoli on that fateful Saturday afternoon, the backroom had undergone a transformation into a courtroom spectacle. A judge's table sat at the end of the room, flanked by benches where members of the stag party could bear witness to the judiciary process, and there, in the middle of the room was a lone seat where, the dastardly condemned would await his judgment.

To add an extra layer of certainty to the verdict, his wedding day best man was ordered to don suitable robes - a bright green mankini and a polka dot bow tie.

Keen to kick things off with a bang, the first charge was unveiled. The crime: making an ex-girlfriend cry.

The BFG was brought forward and handcuffed to the defendant's chair.

"Explain yourself." Was the instruction given.

"There's nothing to explain, I dated her for about a week and then I broke off the relationship."

"Why?"

"Well, I had taken her home after we got talking in the library on night, and one thing let to another, and next thing I know we are in bed having sex."

"What happened next?"

"When we awoke in the morning, I realised that she had a big bottom."

"And what did you do?"

"I told her that I didn't like fat women."

"Burn him!" came the roar from the judgmental crowd.

His defence lawyer valiantly attempted to mount a reasonable defence, seeking clemency from the judge. However, when the star witness—the linchpin for absolving BFG—was presented, even the world's best lawyer couldn't extract sufficient testimony. The star witness? A potted plant. Yep, a leafy friend who refused to spill any evidence in solidarity.

With the inevitable judgment of guilt, the gavel came down, followed by raucous applause from the mob.

"Now for sentencing," I instructed. "Bring in my special guest!"

The atmosphere in the room was electric and with the entrance of the first stripper the cheering erupted.

Clad in black leather, and donning knee-high boots, Miss Whiplash strutted into the room.

In the grand tapestry of mistakes, not checking with the Rude Dog about the type of stripper he had been secured for the afternoon's entertainment was one of them.

You see when Miss Whiplash revealed, and then unleashed her cat of nine tails black whip upon the BFG, it took us all by surprise. But it wasn't long before Miss Whiplash's commitment to the role had left the Stag's back looking like a canvas for a particularly intense abstract painting.

Only Rude Dog knew that Miss Whip Lash was a sexual dominatrix who had been enlisted for the afternoon's entertainment, and no one had given her the memo to take it easy.

After the seventh and eighth full-on swing of the whip, the BFG had finally reached its limit. He declared that if the punishment didn't immediately cease, he would take matters into his own hands.

As the judge, I halted the proceedings, descended from my lofty bench, and whispered sweetly in his ear,

"Let the girl work."

A look of fear descended on the dear man's soul, and in that moment, I felt compassion. I called out to the Rude Dog that the second part of his punishment was now to be revealed.

The music was cranked up, and in walked Nurse Cherry Pie.

A vision of mercy appeared with blonde hair, huge personalities, and wrapped up in a short white dress armed with a stethoscope and a sultry look. She walked straight passed the BFG and started passionately kissing Miss Whiplash.

Miss Whiplash and Nurse Cherry Pie were a dynamic duo, and as they went about making the world right again for the BFG, his quiet sobs of pain transformed into laughter and the previous concerns about a joke gone too far disappeared as quick as the remaining clothes that the ladies still had on.

As the sordid spectacle unfolded in the court room, Rude Dog emerged from the kitchen a meter-long tray of lemon and lime jelly, which had been chilling in his fridge overnight.

Perplexed, I inquired, "How the hell are we going to eat that?"

"It's not for eating," he replied with a mischievous twinkle in his eye.

The jelly found its place on the floor next to the ladies who were now slowly undressing the BFG. It soon became apparent that a jelly wrestling competition was on the horizon, starring the stag and the two ladies.

Now, the unspoken rule is what goes on tour, stays on tour, but what goes on a stag do will forever echo through the halls of stag day lore.

Suffice it to say that the evening unfolded as a resounding success, and that BFG is happily married to this day. But in the annals of Tivoli pub history, that unforgettable evening stands as a testament to Rude Dog's generosity in giving a great mate a send-off from bachelor life that can only be described as fantastically absurd.

What goes on tour stays on tour, until now.

> *Seeing as the Tivoli was no longer in existence, and the university bar was under repair, there was only one real choice left, the Ealy pub, which was an old stomping ground from our past.*

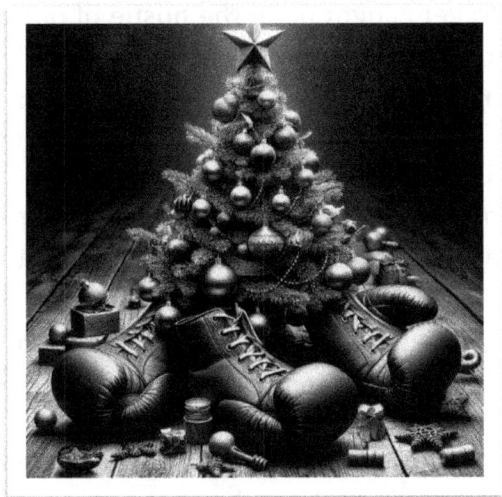

Story 10

Christmas Dinner

The final story in this book is about friendships. Those magical bonds that are like the fine wines of life. Once you find the right crew, it doesn't matter if you're climbing mountains or wrestling Persian invaders; those friendships are your rock, your shield, and your anchor in the storm of life.

Now, these mates don't just show up when the calendar flips to birthdays, Easter, or Christmas. But life has a quirky way of making us sometimes forget the importance of regular friendship maintenance.

We tend to get caught up in the hustle of our daily lives, and its only when memories are jogged that we remember, 'Hey, maybe I should give my pals a shout.'

Enter the friendships forged on the rugged fields of rugby, where camaraderie is thicker than the mud on the pitch. As the years have glided by and we friends find ourselves scattered across the globe like rugby balls kicked in all directions, the memories of the times spent together become treasured presents.

Back in the glorious days of my time at Cardiff, I was fortunate enough to have been made captain of my university side. Bestowed with this honor I set about molding this group of young men into a formidable rugby team who understood the bonds both on the field and off it.

To help in the comradery, it was agreed that each Christmas during our time at university, and for some years afterwards, we would all meet up and celebrate the victories and challenges of the past year.

So, in mid-December we would start the preparation for our annual feast. A gastronomic celebration where we aimed to cook a turkey large enough that it could be mistaken for an ostrich, surrounded by a battalion of peeled potatoes and an army of Brussels sprouts.

Now, as any respectable gathering would have it, our culinary endeavors were paired with crates upon crates of beer, bottles of port, cases of whiskey, and a selection of fine cigars.

Additionally, and to add a touch of sophistication to our revelry, each member of the team would don a tuxedo and cheap chemist-bought aftershave for an added air of class.

And it was on that fateful Christmas evening back in the nineteen nineties when I hosted our annual gala at my student house at 62 Colborn Street, primarily due to the lack of furniture supplied by my landlord, we managed to cram the entire rugby team into our front room.

As preparations unfolded in a whirlwind of culinary chaos, the odds of our turkey being either undercooked or over-cremated stood at a solid sixty percent. The Brussels sprouts had already been vanquished in the fiery furnace of our oven, leaving only the roast potatoes with a glimmer of hope for edibility.

Yet, Christmas, in our hallowed rugby traditions, was less about gastronomic perfection and more about the drinking, stories, and the conquest of Regent Street and Park Lane on the monopoly board through strategic game play.

The dinner party was in full swing, a symphony of laughter and the clinking of glasses. But, in a room packed with 30 large, semi-tamed rugby players, the testosterone levels were threatening to ignite as the monopoly stakes had been heightened following one hotel already being put on Park Lane and accusations of irregular money laundering at the bank.

Sensing the need for a breather, Goldie, Jock and myself decided to head down to the local pub for a Martini, shaken of course, not stirred.

As we, three musketeers, strolled towards the Ely pub, we began weaving tales of the year's escapades, and Goldie began recounting how he had recently won the affections of a striking blonde lady earlier that month.

When he and she were confronted by her ex-boyfriend, who was a member of the Cardiff University math's football team, she had taunted the chap by telling him that she preferred a more muscular rugby man over a member of the football team.

We laughed out loud, as it was clear that our reputation as the most handsome and sexy sporting team had reached legendary status.

Upon entering the Ealy pub that evening, expecting nothing more than a sophisticated drink, we were met with a problem. Lo and behold, the Cardiff University math's football team was having their annual gathering, reflecting on their season's triumphs and tribulations.

A sense of impending doom settled upon us as we locked eyes with them, and we realized that the ratio of eleven to three in favour of them was not good odds if things were to turn physical.

On this occasion, Goldie's exploits in helping to perpetuate the myth that blondes prefer rugby players was not proving helpful, and the football hyenas were already circling, sensing revenge.

The tension escalated steadily over the next ten minutes before the pack finally decided to make their move perpetuated by the fact that a few minutes earlier we had sent Jock, a five foot four Tight-head Prop weighing well over twenty stones, back to the dinner party to summon reinforcements.

As Jock exited the pub, the braver of the pack saw their chance for a frontal assault, and moments later, a pub brawl had begun; a collision of manly pride fueled by a touch of Christmas bravado.

The pub transformed into a battleground, where warriors from two different sporting codes clashed in spectacular style. The air was filled with battle cries, tinsel and all why Christmas songs playing merrily in the background.

Goldie, a seasoned veteran from the military, and myself being a black belt in judo, fueled by drink and a misguided sense of invincibility decided to take on the invading horde armed only with our quick wits and battle-hardened rugby training.

On reflection our decision was not unlike King Leonidas when he decided to face the overwhelming odds when he took on the Persian army at the hot gates.

It seemed like our bold stand might end up with us in the local hospital. But then, in a glorious moment, I landed a remarkable right hook, sending their goalkeeper hurtling across the room.

The bouncers tried to intervene, but with adrenaline still coursing through our veins the battle was not yet over.

We were still the focus of the football players' aggression, and they were eager to give us a Christmas present turned Boxing Day treat.

Amid the impending round two, we shed our dinner jackets, rolled up our sleeves, and embraced the philosophy that if we were going down, it would be swinging. The hyenas circled, ready to give us a good old-fashioned whooping, when suddenly, the heavens opened, and a magnificent sight graced our eyes.

Jock, not the nimblest of rugby players, had that night been possessed with the fleet-footed speed of Hermes, the God of speed and with his kilt flowing in the night's air he had made it back to the rugby house party in record time.

With utter exhaustion, and in his broad Scottish accent, he had burst through the front door, gasping for air, and yelled the words:

"Fight!" before collapsing on the floor.

Although I didn't personally witness the spectacle, as I was about to engage in battle, I can only imagine the awe-inspiring sight of twenty rugby men pouring out of a small, terraced house, called to battle to save their mates.

The Spartans were off to a glorious war, ready to aid their brothers in arms.

Back in the pub, as the close quarter pushing had begun, we braced ourselves for the first blows to land.

We had been backed into the corner of the pub and so the mob were unsighted to the group of huge lads that had just come crashing through the door behind them.

"And what the hell are you smiling at?" came the taunt from one of the chaps.

"Do you know how to scrummage?" I asked.

"What do you mean?"

"Well, before we go to war in a scrum, we follow a very particular set of instructions from the referee."

"What?" the reply came.

Our rugby brothers were now in position just behind the football team and the towering stature of our six foot seven second rowers and our twenty stone props were casting a large shadow that now fell on the hyenas.

"Let me take you through the process – Crouch... Touch... Pause.....Engage!"

And, like the legendary battles of the mighty Spartans, the enemy was laid waste to.

Bodies went flying into the air like ragdolls and the center mass of the enemy formation was crushed under foot as our colossal props drove through the center of the opposition knocking them flying in all directions.

As the new variables in the equation of pub brawling were introduced, the math geeks recalibrated their probability of success in this confrontation.

And as if by heavenly intervention, and at that very moment, Santa entered the pub.

A treat the bar staff had pre-arranged for all the patrons of the pub as a way to celebrate the festive season of cheer and goodwill to all.

A quietness descended on the room, and all that could be heard was the sound of: 'we wish you a merry Christmas and a Happy New Year' coming from the music system.

To break the silence, Santa offered the words:

"Ho Ho Ho...Merry Christmas?"

Giggles started to fill the pub, war was over.

As our merry band of rugby brothers returned to our dinner party accompanied by one of two of the math's football team, bonded by the trial and tribulation of sporting conquests, we basked in the knowledge that enemies are just mates you haven't yet been properly introduced to.

As the night unfolded, we started singing Christmas songs, though perhaps not hitting all the right notes or using the correct lyrics, but there was an unmistakable air of good spirit and lifelong friendships that had been made.

Amidst the merriment, I found myself gazing around at the eclectic assembly of friends who had made their way into my life. The joy and camaraderie we shared were nothing short of magical.

With a beer in hand, I stood up and declared to my companions:

"You know what, mates?"

They raised their eyebrows, anticipating another dose of my infamous rugby pep talks.

"Someday, I'm going to pen down all these adventures and turn them into a book."

Laughter erupted, accompanied by a chorus of skeptical remarks.

"No chance," they chimed. "What goes on tour stays on tour."

"Maybe," I retorted with a mischievous twinkle, "but these tales are just too good to keep to ourselves."

And as I sat there, looking around at my rugby brothers, a smile crept across my face. I was happy with my life's adventures and the friends that I had made.

And as we continued to laugh and share stories, the door opened, and in walked the math's university football team.

"Time for one last adventure"? I asked the team.

To be continued...

Epilogue

Each one of the stories retold in this book is based on a true adventure.

Further, the characters I have described in this book are my real-life friends, albeit I have changed their names to avoid exposing their indiscretions.

Buster, Goldie, Jock, Scooter, Irish, Byson, Mickey, Timmy, Gweebo, Little Elvis, Hedgehog, Lee, and Roo are top blokes who I am happy to have met in my lifetime.

Now, I have only ever retold these stories when catching up with my mates or sharing tales with new friends when pressed to describe what it was like being part of a rugby team back in the 1990's.

And these are just the tip of the iceberg.

However, after much deliberation, and encouragement to share these escapades, I reveal all in this first book a selection of adventures that were just too good to keep to myself.

So, what goes on tour stays on tour, until now.

About the Author

From the rolling hills of Wales, a lover of the game was born.

'Milo', as he's fondly known, embraced the rugby pitch at the ripe age of eight, and the game never quite recovered.

His Sundays transformed from hymns to scrums, and the communal wine was swapped for muddy pints.

Injuries may have tackled his playing days, but they couldn't dampen his spirit. Milo, now turned professional coach, a rugby whisperer of the scrummaging dark arts and front row tactics.

His heart remained on the field, reminiscing the rucks, the mauls, and the mates who turned every match into a page out of folklore.

So here's to Milo, from trading sermons for tries and never looking back, except to chuckle at the shenanigans that made him the man he is today.

www.ingramcontent.com/pod-product-compliance
Lightning Source LLC
Chambersburg PA
CBHW071133090426
42736CB00012B/2111